Habitat

We take for granted that homes today are planned as a series of rooms off shared circulation space just as our current urban planning model is focused around continuous urban blocks that face onto movement corridors in the form of streets. The all-pervading notion that this is the only way to plan our houses and our cities is evidenced in the copious amounts of best practice guidance documents that promote this approach. Whilst these are undoubtedly sound models they are premised on particular notions of social engagement, privacy and security that have been culturally and historically influenced. The analogy between how we move through our city, how buildings sit in relation to that means of circulation and how we move through our home and the relationship to its domestic spaces merits consideration if we are to manage domestic and urban planning as both a methodological and a phenomenological study.

The architectural plan describes the changing nature of human relationships. Until only 100 years ago people were happy to share living quarters with family, colleagues or even strangers. In medieval times sleeping often happened in living spaces typically due to a lack of other options. Gradually some functions such as sleeping have moved into private domains, others such as bathing have found their place in the home having previously been a communal function, whilst others have merged into a shared space such as dining and cooking, these two having been separated from the early sixteenth century through to Victorian times.

Our preference is for buildings to endure longer than the time frames such social tendencies last. The fashion of opening up Victorian properties, linking the kitchen and dining space or re-planning Georgian terrace houses to accommodate an annexe flat or en-suite bathroom bears witness to the need to design for long term flexibility of spaces.

We are not, however, in the business of future gazing. We build on our collective experience of dwellings to create a set of spaces that meet current social structures and needs. Our concern is to ensure that we design for the diversity of needs today. By creating loose fit spaces and long life structures we can allow for future changes without needing to pre-empt every option.

At Mæ we are drawn to three types of domestic spatial configuration:
  *Space with defined territories.
  *An enfilade of spaces.
  *Rooms and corridors.

Each type has its urban equivalent. The first has parallels with the Agora. The second with the medieval monastic planning or the university quadrangle structure and the third with urban block structure as previously mentioned.

The first condition 'Space with defined territories' is almost the antecedent of the house; a single space with zones for different uses defined by furnishings. The most basic being the yurt formed as a single-family space with a central hearth around which rugs and furniture create zones of use. Its spatial qualities are characterised by the overall structural envelope. For us, it represents the most direct means of framing space and creating habitat. For Nikolaus Pevsner it might fall into the category 'building' akin to a shed rather than architecture yet the purity of form, the elegance of the compression wheel and lattice structure, the directness of its layered felt as a thermal envelope and the symbolic meaning of its decoration offer greater clues for architecture than many iconic buildings. The often richly adorned interior demonstrates its suitability for personalisation, adopting the sentimental qualities that make somewhere a home. The home is planned as a single social space where company is the ordinary condition and solitude the exception. Internally, notions of privacy, are dispensed with.

Farnsworth House, interior

Mies van der Rohe recognised when designing the Farnsworth House that we can manage with very few indicators for how to map out and territorialise domestic space. A core containing service installations forms the equivalent of the hearth around which sleeping, dining and living areas are each given definition purely by their furniture. People occupying the house have a permanent visual relationship between one another, whilst privacy from the outside world relies on its remoteness from other buildings and shelter from surrounding woodland.

The model has not lent itself to volume housing and has limited urban equivalents but the Agora of Ancient Greece and the Forum in Rome are worth recognising as being similar for their shared territory with a lack of defined circulation.

The Agora and Forum both refer to central spaces used for public assembly, meetings and discussion. They were a landscape on which

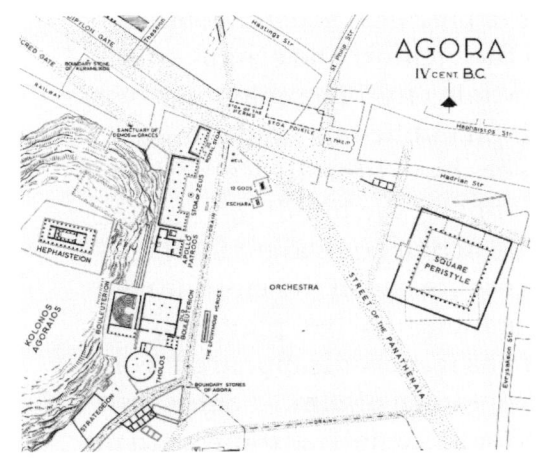

Restored plan of the Agora at the end of the 5th C BC

a series of objects and programmes sit; education, politics, religion, oratory, philosophy, art, and athletics flourished within the urban arrangement.

It is possible to establish parallels between the two in terms of their relationship with the landscape and the way in which the different programmes sit. However, essentially the Agora was responsible for giving the citizens self-consciousness, whereas the Forum is more about a relationship to the state.

With an 'enfilade' of space, resulting plans leave areas of doubt between where inhabitation and transition take place. The loose fit arrangement would seem to prioritise opportunity for unexpected social engagement. Plans based on a matrix of connected rooms are generally opened up for convenience and diverse ways of inhabiting space whilst affording vistas and greater visual, spatial interest.

Palazzo Chiericati, colonnade

Scope for privacy is limited. In a Palladian plan, such as the sixteenth century Palazzo Chiericati in Vicenza, we see a layout in the form of an enfilade of spaces giving spatial interest appropriate to the ideas of visual aesthetics of the time; those that are characterised in perspectival projection.

The Palazzo Chiericati is comprised of a series of rooms where each has more than one door connecting to further rooms, forming a matrix. At the time the tendency was that more doors in a room were preferable leaving no distinction between circulation space and inhabited space. Company is the ordinary condition and the plan encourages paths to cross between all members of the household. The definition of 'served' and 'serving' spaces only appears later. The Palladian plan suited not only the gregarious nature of the members of the household it even goes so far as to extend its footprint to form a colonnade over the Piazza dell'Isola

Habitat

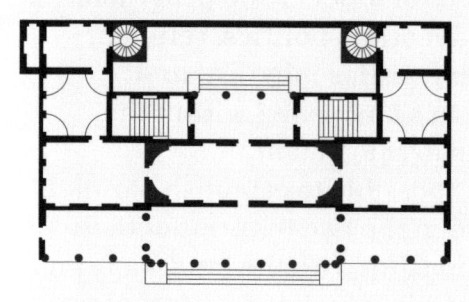
Palazzo Chiericati, plan

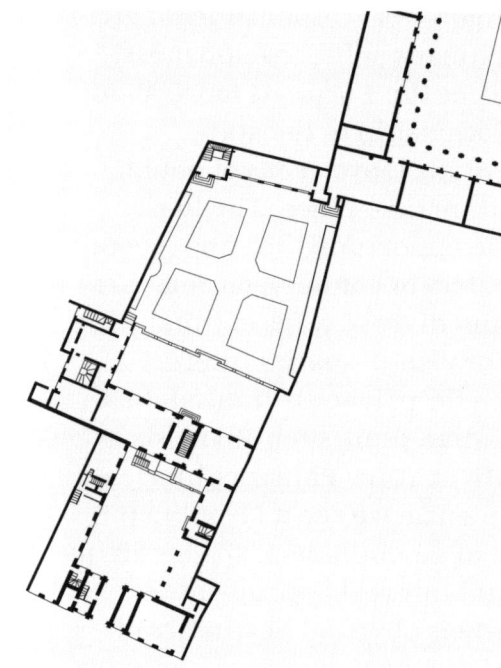
Hôtel Sully, plan

for the patron's "greater comfort and the comfort and ornament of the whole city." The colonnade was built on public land and allows passers by to literally walk through and inhabit the building.

The urban equivalent for us represents one of the most intriguing models of urban planning and has largely disappeared from current town planning; being as it is difficult to deliver today with our habit of distinguishing movement corridors from public spaces, zone land uses and defining public from private. Hôtel Sully in Paris is a 'hôtel particulier' built in 1625. It was designed to connect to the Royal Palace at Place des Vosges and comprises a series of connected courtyards. To move between courts you move through buildings. At Hôtel Sully whilst movement patterns are open to negotiation the expectation is that you move through the middle whilst more passive activities occur around the edges. Equivalent urban models are the quadrangles and courts of Oxford and Cambridge Colleges, which illustrate similar planning although here there is a clear expectation that journeys adopt the long route around the edges; taking their origin as they do from the monastic cloister. Nonetheless the interlocking courtyards afford space to dwell, to move, to encounter. The buildings here form the grid lines and courts form the grid squares rather than the corridor plan explored below where the routes form the lines and buildings fill the grid squares between. Patterns of life are apparently inverted.

'Rooms and corridors' were developed as a means of separating the householder from their servants in the early seventeenth century. This spatial configuration was later recognised as the archetype for residential plans in the Georgian terraced house. It became the

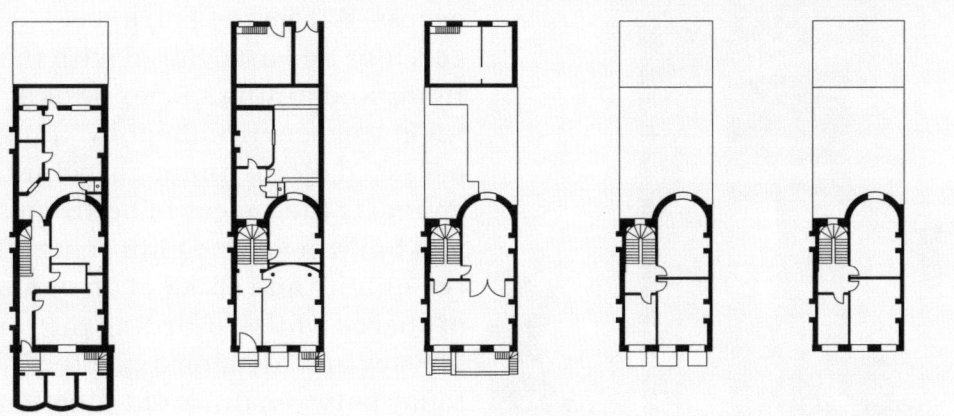

Georgian terraced house, plans

means of securing privacy, comfort and independence. Passageways were introduced into the home to keep the servant out of the way of the householder. Distinguishing route from destination the terminal room off a corridor afforded privacy and retirement. It is today almost indispensible to most domestic planning due to its inscription in Building Regulations as a means of managing egress in the event of fire. The arrangement focuses on function and utility leaving the opportunity for obscure views through a series of rooms removed and social engagement segregated.

Jose Antonio Coderch's apartment building in Barcelona Casa de la Marina, 1952, illustrates how a cellular plan can be developed to achieve spatial qualities that go beyond the simple separation of private rooms off of the circulation space. It adopts a layout where each flat has an entrance lobby and corridor from which rooms are accessed. The lobby gently swells to form space sufficient to take off your shoes, hang up your coat and adjust from an outdoor environment to an indoor environment. The splay of the walls and position of doors direct the eye from the entrance back outside, through either the corner window of the living room or through the middle room to the balcony beyond.

Two doors in the middle room allow it to belong either to the

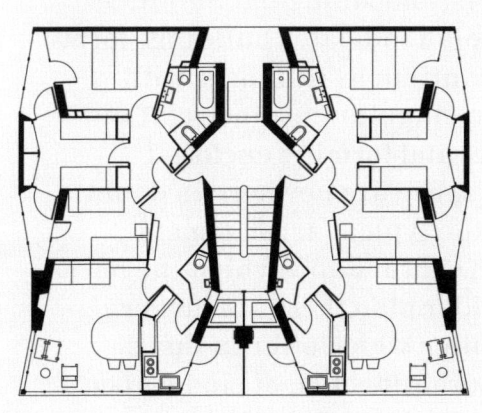

Casa de la Marina, typical floor plan

11   Habitat

Casa de la Marina, apartment hallway

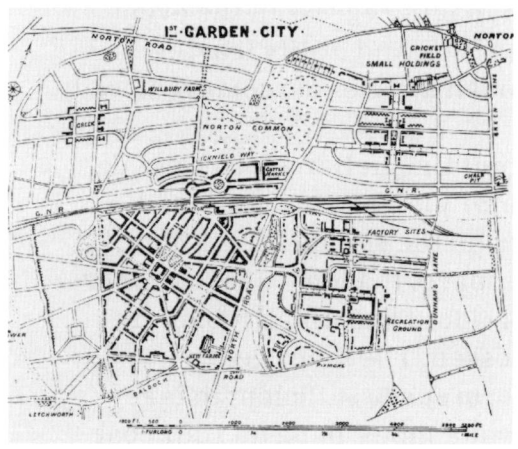

Letchworth Garden City, plan

daytime environment as a study accessed from the entrance corridor and associated with the living and dining spaces or as a night time environment by being accessed off the inner corridor that connects the spaces of bedrooms and bathroom. The plan achieves the quality and spirit of an enfilade of spaces whilst affording the privacy and division expected today between different functions.

Urban equivalents are numerous but I will cite Parker and Unwin's plan for Letchworth Garden City, being a place that we return to at the end the book, and because it represents a model of city planning with similar paternalistic tendencies that considered separating 'serving' spaces from 'served' spaces in the domestic plan as the appropriate moral framework for the nation. The Main Avenue forms the entrance corridor leading from the station off of which are programmed specifically urban blocks: Sites for Public buildings; Sites for Schools; Sites for Places of Worship; Hotels; and Municipal buildings. The plan indicates buildings forming continuous frontages with clear, singular entrances off the street and forming enclosed gardens to the rear. Public and private space are nowhere in doubt.

The matrix of connected rooms was the typical arrangement of domestic space until the seventeenth century and, whilst the norm since the nineteenth has been the corridor plan there are modern equivalents such as Adolf Loos' Villa Müller, which offers a three dimensional matrix of spaces that is more reflective of modernism's preferred isometric projection through the lateral and vertical connection of rooms.

Villa Müller, interior

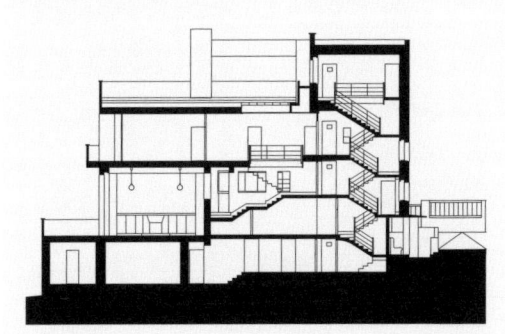

Villa Müller, section

Adolf Loos' own description for Villa Müller demonstrates that his approach was spatial rather than programmatic: "For me, there are only contiguous, continual spaces, rooms, anterooms, terraces etc. Storeys merge and spaces relate to each other". Whilst the plans for Villa Müller note specific uses, even socially segregated uses such as Gentleman's library, Man's dressing or Lady's dressing room, they nonetheless seem to allow more diverse patterns of domestic life than a corridor plan. The rooms within a Palladian villa by contrast are undefined in their use giving little distinction to how the spaces should be inhabited.

We seem to be at a point where lifestyle preferences are tending towards open plan layouts, where our constraints on space are demanding greater flexibility. At an urban scale we have ideas about shared surfaces, homezones, community gardens and cooperatively planned neighbourhoods. Shifting social patterns can help liberate our approach to planning. The fact that the planning of domestic or urban spaces is socially and politically inflected lies at the heart of much of Mæ's thinking. We can develop changes in typical house plans away from the conservatism of Victorian patterns of corridor and terminating room towards hybrids of Raumplan and Plan Libre, and at an urban level we have great opportunity for morphing models of planning, mixing networks of streets with networks of spaces and buildings that form edges or act as objects. The matrix plan with its layers of space provides a format for social life by drawing people together whilst offering enriched spatial experience. As a type we believe it merits being revisited today.

When we design we reflect on the histories that have shaped our city and our houses and draw on this collective knowledge finding work somewhere between memory and invention. We try to combine spatial experiences with recognised methodologies of planning believing that change in architecture happens gradually. For us, radical architecture builds and critiques what went before, but nonetheless we question the forces that shaped those spaces to find new work that is libertarian and generous, and create architectural and urban structures in which change can occur.

Type

> "In the art of architecture, the house is certainly that which best characterises the customs, tastes, usages of a people; its order, like its organisation, changes only over very long periods of time."
>
> *Viollet-le-Duc: Dictionnaire raisonné de l'architecture française de XI au XVI siècle.*

Our office has observed a recent working tendency, shared by many architecture practices, that reconnects with the legibility and human scale of the row house. Plan configurations have been developed independently that have much in common. This is hardly surprising given the common standards we work to. Various sub-types of row house design appear to have coalesced into patterns capable of challenging, we believe, the longevity, urban coherence and adaptability of earlier terrace models.

The row house explored here are examples developed at Mæ. All value architecture as an art of the everyday and thus exhibit respect for their un-named clients. We think that it is impossible to consider the contemporary British row house without some reference to its robust forebear, the Georgian terrace.

The essentials of the speculative Georgian terraced house came into being in a relatively short period towards the end of the seventeenth century. The disposition of single dwelling units arranged in rows, behind unifying street façades, became Britain's most tenacious domestic form well into the nineteenth century. Its familiar plan of two habitable rooms at raised ground floor, with the rear stepping to one side to accommodate a stairwell accessing an extension, a garden or yard, the basement and upper floors, has proved remarkably flexible over the years, while its restrained neo-classical façades occupy a singular place in the life of British and Irish townscapes.

Georgian terraced house, elevations

The constructional economies of the row house envelope, based upon the liberating cleavage of the party wall, existed well before this period. What makes the Georgian terraced house interesting is that speculative dwellings, of similar plan configuration, were considered appropriate for practically all levels of society. While few property owners of this period would have described themselves as democratic (that sort of thing went on in the Colonies or France), the way they chose to live, could at a push, be described as such. Social diversity (demarcation of class, gentility and wealth), was maintained by the level of taste displayed in the design of the façade and detailing and size of dwelling interior.

Arranging row houses in a way that forms edges and frame spaces help urban legibility and orientation of the public realm. Area character and identity as developed through deployment of standard house types need not imply sameness and visual monotony. We believe that the row house is an innately sociable form and as with all gatherings a little variety in the guest list can help the party along. If we look at Bruno Taut's Britz Metropolitan Development, one of the six modernist housing estates of Berlin, he introduces simple shifts in façade geometry, to present a pause in the urban grain. This allows the imposition of a modest but significant external green space. Such an informal moment would appear to be a relative of the green verge or bank found in the Garden City, an acknowledged reference for Taut; it is picturesque in intention but entirely appropriate for an urban setting.

Britz Metropolitan Development

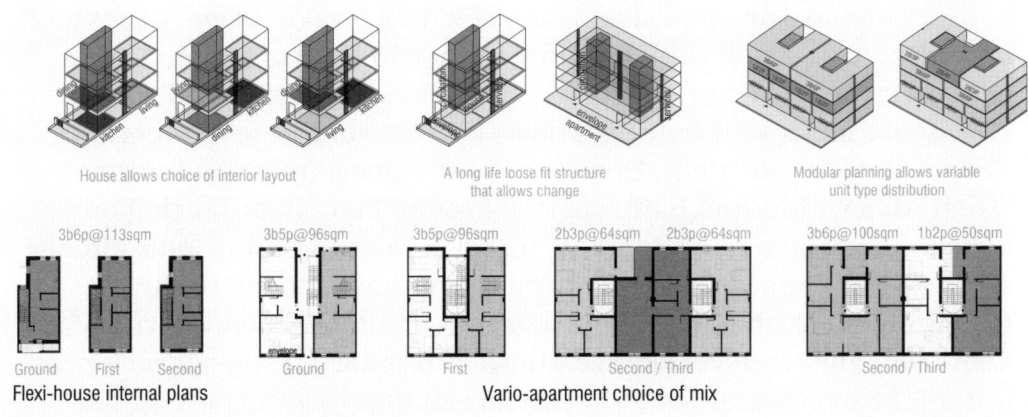

Chobham Manor (competition entry), type plans

Our proposal for Chobham Manor takes the relatedness of various standard plans as the starting point. Variations in material, street line and roof form are suppressed, favouring more subtle changes in rhythm produced by interspersing units of different width and fenestration to enliven the unified street or green space façade and create a sense of place.

At their best Georgian terraced houses—rated First through to Fourth according to their ground rent—were arrayed in a number of ways in any one part of a town: streets, squares and crescents, adjacent to semi-public planted areas and island churches, while the rear mews structures of First Rated dwellings provided further variation in scale and character. The variegated house type and street condition of Chobham Manor owe no small debt to this model. The building lines are never less than efficient, varying between a few metres with a planted buffer zone for larger dwellings facing public areas, to back of pavement for more modest buildings in semi-private mews environments.

The way that row houses survey the realm of the street, is a function of the type of room on ground and first floor, window area and distance from pavement line. Too close, with a sitting room on a slow street and the occupants might feel they are living in a goldfish bowl; too far and the street can feel isolated and un-surveyed. Room function at ground floor front is always governed by plot width, which is usually hostage to the density requirements for any given project, not often pervious to the questioning of lowly architects.

The Georgians managed to pack a drawing room of reasonable dimension and entrance hall on the raised ground level into the modest plot width of 5 to 5.4 metres for a Georgian Fourth Rated house. This gave an open street aspect with a level of privacy provided by a 1.5 metres street setback and a change in level of two to three external steps. The net area of a contemporary row house of, say, 120 square metres for four bedrooms is often similar to its Georgian Fourth Rated equivalent. However the requirements for additional circulation widths and bathrooms at ground floor, in order that our housing stock might be adaptable for an aging population, plus kitchen and gathering spaces mean that room sizes have tended to shrink. It is often impossible to provide a decent habitable room at ground floor front and the level change allowed by external steps is no longer part of the designers' armoury as a means of providing perceptual separation from the street. In combination these issues form a matter of some nicety and designers have to make some tough decisions.

    The terrace with carport adapts the row house for our mobility needs of today. It lends itself to sites where density is not intense enough to merit a car-free approach yet needs to be sufficient to use land efficiently and create a sense of place.

    For our <u>Grow House</u> we considered the car port as an infrastructural component that can enable future change. Here a habitable room in the form of a kitchen-diner can be positioned at the front of the property on the ground floor. Room sizes and set outs are sensible and circulation is kept to a minimum. A living room faces the garden with the potential to connect to a further room in lieu of the carport. With the three bedroom version an enclosure is already formed above the carport making adaptation straightforward.

    The ability to park on site, an advantage to tenants or owners, has to be paid for with an increase in envelope and therefore construction cost. Something that not all clients, or more importantly for social housing projects, contractor or developer partners are willing to countenance. Their costs are usually based on a survey of surrounding existing property values, without taking into account the value addition that a well-designed neighbourhood can deliver. Yet when weighed against the cost and upheaval of moving the value of building

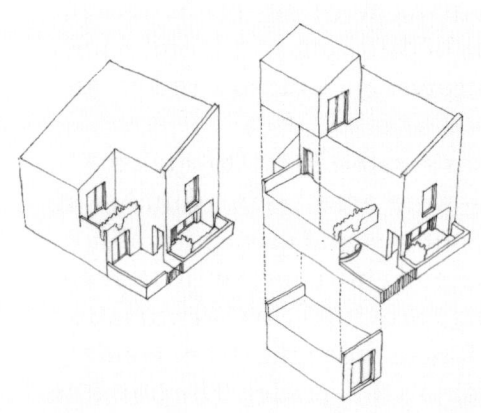

<u>Grow House</u>, transformations

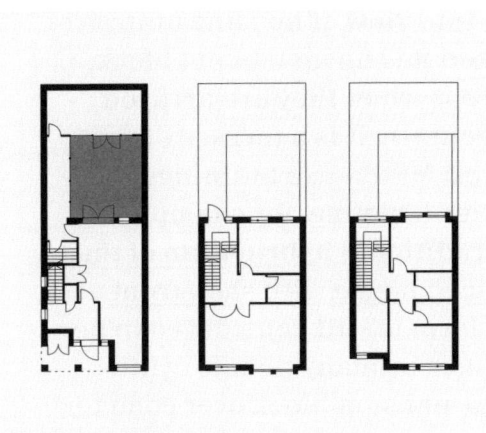

Piano Nobile House, plans

in an infrastructure for future expansion seems worthwhile.

The Courtyard type of plan is a relative of the Carport type, however we have separated them where the relationship with the car does not exist or is diminished by the inclusion of a garage. Our proposal for Piano Nobile House are by far the largest of the dwellings we have developed, with a three storey townhouse at the front of the plot connected to an annex accommodation at the rear. The buildings' sectional relationship to its Georgian First Rated ancestor is intended.

External space commences with a courtyard garden at ground floor between the dining space and the annex. This opens out on the first floor forming a common ground between the first floor living room and the roof of the annex building. Its variant plan has an additional terrace provided at first floor on the street side, the void in the façade along with the glazed first floor bay windows and steel balustrade balconies help to add gravity to the terrace front as a whole.

Hybrid form of the terraced house with shop front, Calabria Road

In our designs for Chobham Manor, variegation is intentional; it allows a number of unit sizes to occupy the same street. This variety is a virtue in itself; by helping to place larger families alongside young couples, for example, a neighbourhood becomes a more viable social mix from the outset. Adaptability is an additional socially sustainable factor for this project. Addition and adaptation to the rear of the dwelling is enabled. Façade unity is maintained by a common eaves height and building line.

The question of what defines a row house exercises our office from time to time. We generally agree that when single function buildings

Ones own front door, Agar Grove

Transition between the public and private, Agar Grove

hove into view, if housing units are stacked it is an apartment block, whereas when they are arrayed horizontally it is a terrace of row houses. Mixed-use buildings are trickier to define, for example the traditional hybrid form of the terraced house with shop front. This form is still considered to be a 'house' by many people, while a 1910 mansion block over commercial space, or an interwar parade of shops with deck—accessed horizontally arrayed dwellings are not.

We are currently working on the hypothesis that the definition of 'house' in this instance is cultural (generic British with a strong English twist), and flows from the charming idea that house or home is a place of privacy and by implication personal freedom. This is based upon an idea of individual property ownership, which has a strong memory of owning the land on which the property is built. Based upon nothing more scientific then conversations with people in pubs, a sense of 'house' seems to have a lot to do with ones' own front door. A front door that marks a clear transition between the public and private without the intersession of shared communal space, stairwells and decks.

The space behind the front door is amenable to a certain amount of stretch. As long as the stairs are internal and not shared, people don't seem to mind walking up to the accommodation and still call their dwelling a 'house'. The Warner Half House and its contemporary the Tyneside flat are the familiar model for stacked properties presented as houses.

Warner Half House

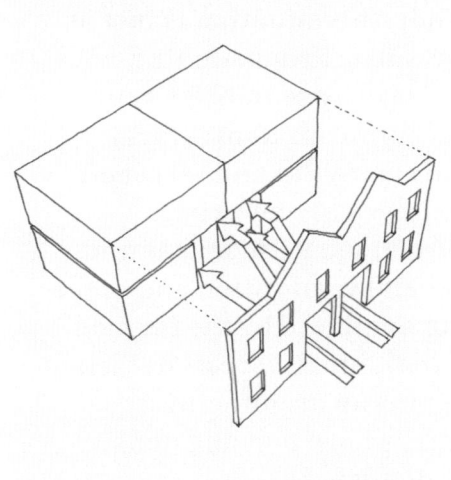

Stacked properties of Warner Half House

Three floors are probably the maximum this idea of 'house' can be pushed to. The first barrier to addition is, we believe, perceptual and based upon the number of flights one is required to climb before encountering habitable space. The second is the increasingly poor ratio of private circulation to dwelling space accrued. Up to three floors the ratio of 20% vertical circulation to dwelling is comparable to a communal stair for a three-floor apartment block. The benefit of this approach, aside from giving residents a greater sense of control over their living environment, is the removal of all internal public space thus reducing maintenance costs for building management agencies.

In addition to including vertical stacking as part of the row house family we would like to refer to examples of semi-attached and the

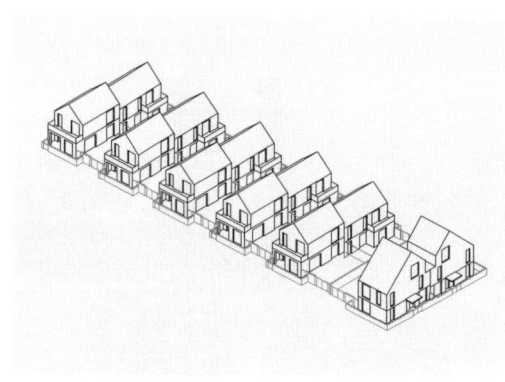
New Islington, axonometric

single house terrace form. Our intervention at New Islington is a "gappy" sort of terrace, able to maintain its urban presence through the proximity of apparently individual units. The binary rhythms produced by this sort of plan, where two houses are attached by the rear party wall, herald the possibility of semi-attached or completely detached form of terrace.

There are a number of practical reasons for wishing to include open-sided dwelling types in the terrace canon, not least of which would be to allow natural light and ventilation to rooms like bathroom and utility spaces which, unlike Georgian precedent, are so often trapped in the centre of the plan due to the requirements of narrow plots. This issue becomes more acute for larger social housing units, where the additional sales value per square metre associated with the detached or semi-detached label are not always available, and issues of fuel poverty are often pressing.

The civilities required for interactions between individuals are more important the closer they live together; this situation is just as important for buildings in dense urban settings. Proportioning devices such as the traditionally sanctioned change in brick type, hard-fired at ground level with softer, lighter forms above, form a plinth or rustication course for both the semi-villa and terraced form allowing visual connection were no physical one exists.

A unified row of villas or terraces interspersed with pauses and changes in rhythm offer opportunity for social variegation and place making. The restraint and urban decorum exhibited by the terrace of row houses is enlivened by the rugged individuality of its detached relative. In exchange the detached form gains an architectural coherence, which makes it fit for urban life, where housing density requirements might otherwise ensure its demise.

Place

There are certain conditions of cities that form a common DNA. The way that we organise ourselves, facilitate interaction and trade, create boundaries, and find common ground lead to patterns of inhabitation. These patterns are defined by paths, landmarks, edges, nodes, which help to make our cities legible. Many of these universal conditions can be codified to form a set of tools for architects to use. In Mæ's work we consider how codes and patterns that can be categorised through computational methodologies assist or hinder design opportunity and ask what the implications are for the people that we design for?

Figure-ground plan, London

Figure-ground plan, Manhattan

Figure-ground plan, Rome

We are mindful, however, that our cities owe as much to the history, political and the social context of their culture. We know that no two cities are the same, these universal conditions and a city's architecture is inflected by the social and economic exchanges as well as topography and climate. The intensity and variety of a city helps us recognise our place in a broader society of strangers. The buildings that we design at Mæ and our ideas about urban design are informed by these contexts, which in turn contribute to the creation of a sense of place. Our interest is in balancing the generic and the specific; common strategies against specific detail perhaps.

The universal conditions of the city, seen consistently in figure-ground plans across the world, are features such as a connected network of streets, character areas defined by their building types whether civic and institutional or everyday, accessible public spaces that take on meaning through their use, private spaces enclosed by built form and so on.

In this essay we explore the idea of city building and place-shaping in three projects. Our masterplan for Nordhavnen depicts an entirely new place; the Tybalds Estate by contrast aims to add coherence to an existing neighbourhood through new interventions whilst our work at Agar Grove re-models a piece of city.

Our proposal for an urban extension to the city of Copenhagen is a place made up of universal components. These create an infrastructure that can accommodate local and specific patterns.

Nordhavnen is planned as one of the greatest and most ambitious metropolitan development projects in Scandinavia for years to come. Nordhavnen is a 200-hectare area currently used for a number of harbour-related activities. The site will be home to a sustainable urban extension with a development footprint of around three million square meters.

Our focus was to create a series of districts, each with nodes of intensity. We started by asking what the components of a sustainable place are. Each district would have a range of building types, uses and activities needed to meet the demands of everyday life, a variety of spaces for play and leisure nuanced around characteristics of topography and aspect. The density of these components would fall away from the centre.

Nordhavnen (competition entry), masterplan

We think proximity and density play an important role in creating a viable and sustainable neighbourhood. In Delirious New York, Rem Koolhaas defines the metropolis as a 'culture of congestion'. Like Jane Jacobs, his description of the city celebrates the busy hustle in which citizens enjoy anything, anywhere, at any time. Intensification is not just about pushing houses closer together but must be about achieving a sense of place and the creation of local distinctiveness that is attractive to buyers, with a range of services and amenities.

Density results in propinquity, that is the proximity of uses which in turn reduces our reliance

Coded building types, Nordhavnen

on the car, which allows us to spend more time at home or with our friends or pursuing leisure activities.

At Nordhavnen, we developed a simple set of coded building types for residential and commercial use that could achieve different densities and a strategy for their distribution. We deployed computational methodologies to rapidly test resultant massing scenarios from these set of design codes and typologies. We used a grid as the basis for the urban structure and identity. The grid belongs in the realm of the ideal and is associated with a democratic enlightened outlook. We recognise that cities are as much shaped by people's actions and as they are by architects and urban designers. The grid is loose fit to allow change, and can be enriched by local topography.

The resultant plan has defined neighbourhood centres, it has areas of concentration for schools, amenities and services and then a more loosely defined periphery. However, with its simple palette of building typologies, it is what this gridded framework allows that is important to us. The grid can be cultivated before any development takes place—with allotments, market gardens or forest. Landscapes are able to grow food, generate energy, stimulate and sustain employment. Over time, in response to the needs of the city, grid squares can be developed according to the code—though a rich landscape has already established itself on the streets or any grid squares left for public space.

City building has an ethical dimension. We sought to link the development and its planning with their attendant social responsibilities, proposing a Nordhavnen Parliament to oversee local governance and enable citizen participation. Its remit was to act locally whilst thinking globally—supporting residents while promoting itself internationally. As part of the proposal the Nordhavnen Parliament publishes a Citizens' Charter setting out its vision for sustainable development.

As Nordhavnen grows, a place develops that is environmentally responsible and socially diverse: 'a place to start and a place to stay'.

The Charter offers a simple set of ten sustainable principles that developers, residents or businesses are expected to signup to when moving to Nordhavnen. The charter promotes strategies for developing social infrastructure for health and happiness as well for energy production, recycling, local food production and fair trade. It encourages people to live sustainably and build a sense of urban community.

More often than designing from scratch, our work involves enhancing existing neighbourhoods. Here, opportunities for placemaking demand that we interface with existing buildings and add legibility to an established place. New additions are integrated in a way that stitches and repairs the often-fragmented layers of development, and mediates between different historical narratives.

At the time of writing, Mæ are working on two projects that seek to repair the image of the city at a local level. The designs have been developed collaboratively with other architects as well as through a series of design workshops with the planning authority. In the planning workshops, rather than focusing on what policy says or asks of us, we consider first and foremost what is appropriate, how we can build on the history of the place and respond to varied contexts.

At the Tybalds Estate[1] in Holborn, London, we encountered a fragmented neighbourhood. Two isolated towers, built in 1965, sit surrounded by the backs of buildings. Surrounding the towers are Georgian terraces and 1950s slab blocks.

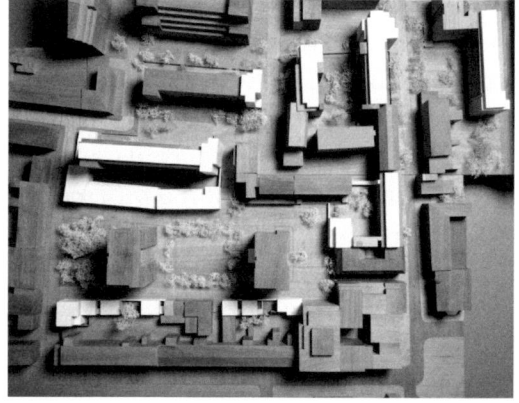
Tybalds Estate, model

The scheme comprises a number of additions: mews houses, a terrace, an apartment block, extensions and overbuilds, which retrospectively integrate the towers into a street scene. We found and added to conditions which we sought to preserve: an existing play area, which we have framed with new buildings, thereby bringing the one of the towers into conversation with the terrace opposite; a mature

Tybalds Estate, Orde Hall Street view

1   Tybalds Estate, London Borough of Camden, designed in collaboration with Tibbalds, Duggan Morris Architects, Avanti Architects and Camlins Landscape Architects

tree that offered a moment of relief between the new houses; a garden wall that we extended to form courtyard houses. There are moments of proximity and adjacency where we chose to step the building line to protect a sense of amenity.

There are conditions that currently don't work, which we can improve upon—such as low levels of communal surveillance remedied through new frontages. Also a poor quality public open space that we offer greater specificity by forming a resident garden and a new apartment building to enclose it. A dead space to the rear of a slab block becomes a new community space.

The project continues our interest in how new architecture can make a place and stitch together different urban conditions. The Tybalds Estate has grown over time, accruing Georgian terraces, modernist towers and 1950s slab blocks. The new buildings aim to pull these together.

The architecture reflects our premise that housing forms the backdrop to our city and its public spaces, and that such a varied texture can be familiar. The buildings are simply expressed and designed to complement the surrounding buildings and the proposed landscape. We have concentrated on the qualities that we believe make for good housing—dual aspect, large windows for good light into the home, generous spaces, outdoor amenity in the form of terraces and balconies, energy efficient, robust and high quality materials.

We have many areas in our cities where the urban fabric is fragmented, where utopian ideas from different eras cause ruptures in the continuity of our streets and spaces. These offer great opportunities to intensify our cities, delivering new and sustainable housing and through close observation make sense of an area's differences.

The London Borough of Camden's approach at Tybalds Estate builds on the legacy of Sydney Cook from the 1960s and 70s where a local authority shows great commitment to the value of good design and demonstrates the role a landowner can take in creating sustainable models of growth and change.

The third project the Agar Grove Estate[2] for the same borough is an estate that sits apart from its

Agar Grove Estate, plan

Place

2   Agar Grove Estate, London Borough of Camden, designed in collaboration with Hawkins\Brown and Grant Associates

context. Our proposal also explores ideas of identity and urban continuity. Agar Grove Estate was constructed by the London Borough of Camden in 1966. The existing buildings are in poor condition and the public space is underused. The estate was constructed at a time of great optimism and certainty. Planned around solar orientation and technical efficiency, the original development sought originality over other values such as memory, familiarity or a responsibility to its wider setting.

Our proposal replaces the existing low-rise buildings with new housing, while an existing tower will be comprehensively refurbished. The design aims to extend the wider condition of the city into the site and amplify the character of the place. Although the existing estate benefits from extensive green space, it lacks definition and is poorly used. Our proposal frames new public spaces enclosing them as you would a room. A new square extends an existing grove of trees on the main street, bringing into conversation the 1950s slab blocks across the street which are matched in scale with a new building.

Historic street patterns are reintroduced helping to stitch in and connect the streets and building form to its context. Our intention is to make it feel seamlessly part of the urban fabric. A new street is formed to open up a connection to the refurbished tower and new buildings positioned to give the tower meaning in the new urban pattern. The new buildings face the tower creating an active streetscape and new public square at the entrance to the tower.

The proposals look to continue the urban character of the Camden conservation area to the north of the site. Not in a literal sense but drawing on the type, the scale, the rhythm and the urban pattern of the context to develop new houses that accommodate the need for diversity and flexibility expected today. The new buildings draw on a typology of houses in the area: terraces, villas and mansion blocks create well-defined urban blocks. Garden walls link the buildings and afford glimpsed views to enclosed green spaces beyond. The scheme will house a mix of tenures including private, shared ownership and social rent as well as some commercial elements in the form of a café, a local shop and business spaces.

Whilst we recognise our duty to the city we are also mindful of our duty to the citizens we house. Our desire to create integrated mixed tenure neighbourhoods is a part of that. The paternalistic and reformist approach to early council housing, replacing the worst of the slums, delivered housing for the poor set apart from speculative builders who dealt with the better-off. The injustice of segregation

Agar Grove Estate, elevation

was noted in 1946 by Aneurin Bevan, minister for both health and housing, who told Parliament:

"You have castrated communities. You have colonies of low income people, living in houses provided by the local authorities, and you have the higher income groups living in their own colonies. This segregation of the different income groups is a wholly evil thing, from a civilised point of view... It is a monstrous infliction upon the essential psychological and biological one-ness of the community."

Today our projects cater for diversity and we have engaged with existing leaseholders, tenants and local residents alike. Listening to local peoples' issues, learning about the community, recording ideas and local experiences, and encouraging design involvement has helped us square our responsibilities to those being rehoused whilst accommodating the general and unknown expectations of new and unknown residents who will add to the population here and build a sense of urbanity.

'Urbanity' demands that we have a social, economic and political engagement with the city; as Richard Sennett notes, it allows us to make use of the density and differences in the city to find a more balanced sense of identification on the one hand with

Agar Grove Estate, terrace and mansion block

Place

others who are like us but also a willingness to take risks with what is unliked, unknown. The city creates space of diversity where difference is privileged.

We like this premise. A city isn't just a place to live or shop—it's a place that implicates how one derives one's ethics and develops a sense of justice. Our role as urban designer is to offer up a coherent physical and social infrastructure that enables a community to develop as they see fit. The architect is merely the facilitator, an agent of change helping residents take control of their own environment.

October 18, 2013

S B   So would you agree that Mæ's work comes from an analysis of sociopolitical systems, but moreover, a close observation of context?

A E   Our architecture is largely informed by observation of the city and buildings we've visited, passed through or lived in, yes. We try to make casual observations as a way of understanding the rich variety of the landscape, drawing on what Honoré de Balzac described as 'the gastronomy of the eye'. Mostly our observations are material but they're also about recognising how we live in cities, how architecture can be civil and urbane and how we relate to the public realm.

S B   Richard Sennett argues that the public realm is a place for strangers to gather. It enables certain kinds of freedoms, and offers people a chance to lighten the pressures of conformity. All of which would suggest that a healthy city embraces difference.

A E   I'd agree with that. Placemaking is about creating neighbourhoods

that people can identify with but they should also be open and generous enough to let strangers in. Recently when masterplanning an estate regeneration, the scheme was criticised by the local police officer as a place that 'allows a person legitimate reason to loiter; that is, a stranger to the area would be permitted to be in the area, without reason.' Their argument was that it would 'reduce surveillance as the residents will not know a person using the route.'
As architects we work between these worlds of tension. On the one hand we want to create places where people belong, feel comfortable, where they might feel a sense of ownership and would project their own identity through personalisation. At the same time, we rally against exclusion
and parochialism. Strangers, we think, should have a right to loiter,
without being perceived as a threat..

MH   In a way we're just talking as familiar strangers now…the first time that Shumi and I ever really encountered each other was through the Architects' Journal and probably at the time of the RIBA Housing show...

Evolving Norms of British Housing exhibition catalogue

S B   That's right – that would be around 2008, at the Evolving Norms exhibition.

M H   That was, I think, one of the things that probably helped us gather pace... it was a good moment. That time was about trying to be conscious of where we were within one generation of architects and practices – maybe a generation and a half – in which we felt we stood in the middle.

A E   In working on the Evolving Norms exhibition, we selected architects who were dealing with similar sorts of issues, similar problems. Issues that ranged from how to create good ordinary housing, through to how to create an architecture that said something about the city and how to design good spaces whilst also battling with policy requirements.

MH   We would share ideas informally with our contemporaries, often in heated pub conversations revolving around these conflicts. Suddenly policy wasn't a constraint so much as an opportunity. And there was a kind of fun about that; it was an arms race or something, um, about…the joy of design.

AE   We all had housing projects on the drawing board but we wanted to talk about them in a wider context. As participants in the broader exhibition, we exhibited Hammond Court as a project that responded to its place. The architecture reframed the Warner houses that surrounded the site, re-imagining them for higher density.

SB   Can we talk about your ideas

of how architecture contributes to neighbourliness?

Street view of Hammond Court opposite Warner terraced housing

A E   Architecture doesn't have all the answers...But we can attempt to design spaces that integrate into existing fabrics and hopefully enable neighbourliness. Ultimately, though, there is so much more at play; partly it's down to management, partly down to how society responds. So for example in Hammond Court, part of the garden is given over to a community food growing initiative and it seems to be working well, there are examples like Bonnington Gardens in Vauxhall or recent pop-up gardens in left over spaces, created by ad-hoc community initiatives. They're fantastic, but they reveal the limit to which architects can facilitate a community.

M H   That project had all the complex challenges that are the familiar hallmarks of housing projects: mixed tenure, a really complex mix of unit types owing to the needs of the returning residents, good space standards, environmental standards and lifetime homes, all within a tight budget.
      Architects of our generation often get the sort of work where there's something 'septic' on site. This was one of those places, beleaguered with a bunch of leaky modernist blocks. They sort of blew apart the neighbourhood, not just in functionality but in the way that the neighbourhood regarded itself. I think maybe the strongest bit of the renewed Hammond Court is the architecture of the street, which functions much better than the original stuff, better on so many levels. In much the same way as the surrounding Warner homes, these fantastic terraces sometimes act as housing blocks and

sometimes as middle class terraces: they strove to blur the issues.

A E   The typology of Hammond Court – and I think also its materiality, and formality – means you can in fact wander past the site of our block, such that it feels part of the continuity of the neighbourhood. You don't have to avoid it; it is in fact just part of the neighbourhood.

M H   If we roll back to the Smithsons' generation of architects – I think that generation were designing for something that they saw as a highly collectivised society. Much of that was forged in the 1890s and 1910s co-operative and socialist movements – everything from effing brass bands! – and you know, that's fantastic. But I think that people thought they could carry on relying on a collective sense of society: neighbourliness forever, but without actually facilitating it. So post-war, you get housing that doesn't actually allow any point where those things, those bits of social glue can evolve, develop and then get to work, so that it extends beyond the allotment society or the amateur dramatic society. We believe in those virtuous circles, and a lot of politicians talk about it now whether it works or not, but I think in housing design you've got to leave space for that stuff.

A E   With quite a few of our projects we're designing for an existing community. For example North Prospect, an estate regeneration in Plymouth, where there was a proposal by the local authority to demolish and re-build the neighbourhood. Consultation wasn't managed well and there was huge opposition, so we were brought in to work more closely with the affected residents. We needed to set out what the minimum parameters were, where something had to happen. Their houses were falling down and they needed investment, the shops had closed down and there wasn't the critical mass to support the local services. Through workshops and walking tours, we were better able to understand which places were important to them and where the problem parts of the estate were – up until then residents had thought that these where beyond repair.

    The other thing that changed their mindset was being transparent about finances. To pay for the refurbishment, the council had to generate a certain sum, and that needed to come from the land – so we developed this board game called 'Prospectopolis' where residents could lay tiles of development. We were able to show what the revenue generation was and then they could see how much had to change in order to refurbish. It just became a very direct, transparent way of communicating. Ostensibly, our role was to take this information and translate it into a masterplan, but for me our main role was realised as architect-enablers, rather than as authors.

M H There's a whole industry involved in consultation now. It's absolutely part of architectural practice today and actually, a part of the job that an architect must be really critically aware of. There's a lot of language about neighbourliness and consultation in architecture, but I think the only way of doing it well is by having an agenda yourself, a really strong one. To go back to where we were, Mæ has a very strong agenda about how it sees us living with our fellow man.

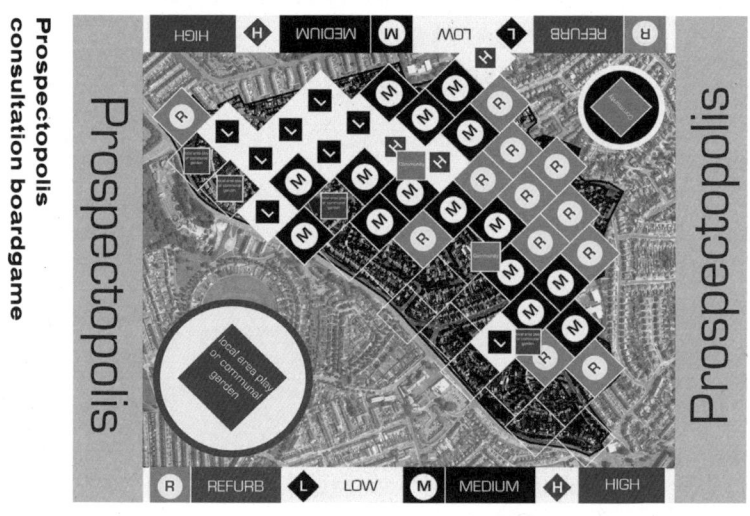

Prospectopolis consultation boardgame

A E   We try to make work that is legible, that says something about the city and engages with the social context that we design in. Let's think of an example... Our project at Lisson Grove, for instance, aims to communicate at a number of levels with the people who will use the building or pass by it.

M H   Is that the tower for the elderly? Now, there's a lucrative sector — we'll all

be there soon enough, if we're lucky.
I mean, we've got a looming crisis
with all the baby boomers reaching
pensionable age; UK pensioner
numbers will grow to something like
four million over the next 25 years...

A E   The tower is part of it...The Lisson
Grove development is like a Lifetime
Neighbourhood across two buildings.
We have an elderly persons' HAPPI
housing scheme, with an employment
space below; a health hub, which
has everything from community café,
crèche, GP practice, dental surgery
and clinical health services, and then
some family housing next door.

S B   That's quite a lot to introduce!
Firstly, can you tell me a little bit about
the difference between HAPPI housing
and Lifetime Homes.

A E   HAPPI principles were developed
to address how architecture can
support people in old age. These
principles go further than those for,
say, Lifetime Homes, which deal
primarily with matters of accessibility.

Whereas HAPPI looks at the social structure that's also needed, communal lounges, gardens, care support.
It suits our concerns about the wider social structures around housing.

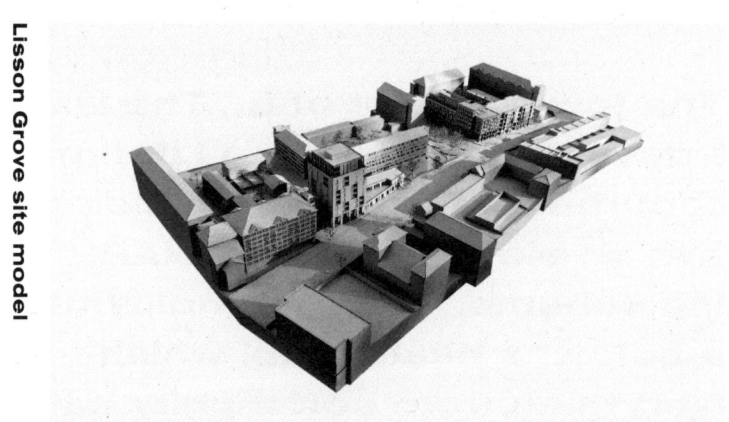

Lisson Grove site model

S B   So, formally, how do you maintain a sense of legibility between such a diverse scheme, and the existing local context?

A E   In this case, it's to do with massing, allowing for a variety of ways to encounter and approach the new development. The site for the older person housing scheme is strategically positioned at an apex on Lisson Grove. It's awkwardly wedge-shaped, mediating between the geometry of the Lisson Green

Estate and the building opposite, which follows the alignment of the street. The community health hub will be developed later on the adjacent site, which currently faces a small green popular with residents pausing to chat on their way to or from Church Street Market.

So we have these interesting conditions. The tower acts a point of orientation, sitting on a main axis commanding a view directly down the road, whilst its podium mediates between the competing site geometries and changes in levels. The health hub terminates one end of Church Street, while Schmidt Hammer Lassen's City of Westminster College caps off the other end. We felt that this building needed to have as much of a presence as that one. The two mark the edges of this amazingly vibrant bit of city.

Lisson Grove, a point of orientation

S B   It feels like a deliberately dense programme on a constrained site. Is it the first phase of a broader development?

Lisson Grove, the Health Hub

A E   Yes, it'll mark the first phase of the wider Church Street regeneration. There's a masterplan that maps out opportunities across the wider area for new housing, social infrastructure and public realm improvements. Most of the opportunities are just fragments of the city but Westminster City Council, our client want this project to be a marker for change, and for the area – demonstrating that architecture can be about both continuity and progress. It's not just a political act though. Of course the project depends on political support to make it happen, but it's fundamentally about the citizen and the user.

S B   So that was my next question; what was your consultation process like? How do you ensure that sense of continuity, while at the same time addressing emerging needs?

A E   This project went through a referendum with 87% support from voters. We have an amazing group of residents that we are working with, particularly the elderly people we are housing. Lisson Grove is designed to give the residents greater independence and enabling them to stay in a home or area that they might feel to be their own for longer, before needing extra residential care. A tower form helps that with easy lift access, short corridors and great views. We're drawn to Eric Lyon's mantra that 'The test of good housing is not whether it can be easily built but whether it can be easily lived in'.

October 23, 2013

S B   So, we were talking about neighbourliness last time we met; I think we can go on with that.

A E   Part of our duty to the city is to engage with the spaces which surround the buildings we create. Public realm underpins the structures of community and creates free spaces for encounter. Earlier this year, I was in Berlin looking at the Groß-Siedlung housing schemes. With projects such as Britz Metropolitan development by Bruno Taut or Siemensstadt by Hans Scharoun, what immediately stands out is not only the quality of the planning and architecture, but also the sheer quality of the landscaping. It is used structurally to frame and enclose spaces, to terminate streets, to complement the architecture. Every garden was planted with two fruit trees and those are still very much in evidence.
    The aspect across garden boundaries at Britz is very open, allowing neighbours to chat, very similar to Vauban in Freiburg. Now, that works brilliantly there, but it demands a cultural willingness to live like this. I can

imagine this sort of open-ness could potentially work on a custom-build neighbourhood where the residents have been working together through the whole process.

M H   ...whereas in the UK we tend to have a dice-and-slice approach, which prioritises private space over public. A certain American[1] said, 'Good fences make good neighbours', and it seems that one of the keys to neighbourliness, in our cities, is really effing well-built party walls and fences.

> 1   Robert Frost in his poem 'Mending Wall' 1914

S B   So speaking of that kind of cultural tension, let's talk about New Islington. That one was interesting because you were inserting an existing community into a new development, weren't you?

A E   It's a bit like the hedgehog dilemma: if a group of hedgehogs come together too closely for warmth in winter, they risk hurting one another. At the Guts in New Islington, we thought about how to bring houses together to form a collective identity, whilst affording families their sense of privacy. We were designing for returning residents of the old Cardroom Estate. Some would already know a few of their neighbours but there were new residents moving into the development too. The design and layout allows loose bonds to form without forcing intimacy.

M H   I think we could probably go back to the fact that we both kind of like the Smithsons. The Smithsons, whether you agree with individual bits of their analysis or not, illustrated ideas about where it was that people could meet and talk in their projects – where they made semi-public space. There's something so immensely charming about that.

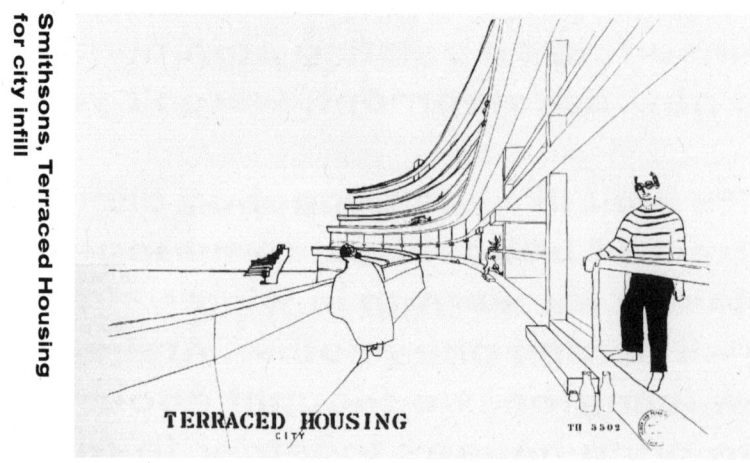

Smithsons, Terraced Housing for city infill

S B   On the raised steps up to the front door, for example, or in front of shared amenities...

M H   I think their methodology is very good, partly because it means you can cut to the chase very quickly. The Smithsons were drawing upon an existing condition and trying to make it legible. We had a lot conversation about condition and how to describe it — what might be desirable to foster, and how one might achieve it through design: this is kind of within the architect's skill-base.

A E   The Smithsons would focus on particular scenarios — the need for enclosure, or the relationship to the street — all questions of micro-architecture. Whereas they seemed to overlook that need for intimacy at a neighbourhood level, they did seem to get behind the idea of keeping the numbers who share a landing or a street to a reduced level, which in turn makes it easier to get to know your neighbours. By contrast, our conversation with Geoffrey Darke revealed a real sensitivity in Darbourne & Darke's work to these issues.

S B   This was at the Architecture Foundation wasn't it? Tell me a bit about that encounter.

A E   We were invited by Ellis Woodman, then the editor of Building Design to interview Geoffrey Darke — this was in 2007. We knew their work previously but it wasn't until that conversation that we really went out and looked at Lillington Gardens and the Aberdeen Park scheme they did in Islington. At the time I was actually living in one of their estates, the Marquess Estate in Islington, perhaps an example of where their aspirations didn't necessarily follow through — but with Lillington Gardens in Pimlico and Aberdeen Park, there is a sort of domesticity in scale that I think works. A lot of it is to do with the humanity of the architecture and the quality of the public realm — the gardens at the back of Lillington, for example, or the communal green in the middle of Aberdeen Park.

M H Darbourne & Darke probably wouldn't have used the term condition at any point; that's not how they communicated to each other or their fellows. But I think that we definitely considered it, we would draw strip cartoons of conditions; sometimes they were romantic, of someone saying hello to someone at the front door or something like that.

Darbourne and Dark, Aberdeen Park

A E Or looking at the relationship of indoor space to outside or chatting over the garden fence.

MH We considered that all of this stuff should be functional kit. We figured that every part of a building has to function around conditions, around doors and fences; it has to be supportive. The Smithsons could rely on an isotropic, post-war society, where there was a large upper working class and a large lower middle class; there was pretty much full employment, everyone got married fairly young, had a kid or two. They could rely on there being a woman at home, kids at school and papa out at the factory or office and so I suspect that the problems of scale that showed up at Robin Hood Gardens much later were not anticipated. Britain after the war was a socialist country in many respects and it was a product of socialist planning. This contrasts with certain things that we were looking at contemporaneously. I lived in certain estates, Alex lived in certain estates and we found we couldn't rely on an idealised family, or an idealised condition within. It was noticeable that the points where these things fell down coincided with the points where the occupancy was wrong.

A E   As an architect you're trying to manage that potential conflict; you want to enable the best to happen but then there's always that risk of unintended outcomes that could lead to less social behaviour.

S B   Maybe we could talk a bit about how you mitigate that – the gestures in New Islington and at Agar Grove too, in terms of neighbourliness and adjacencies...

M H   I think the thing that we found useful was that we had developed a box of tools. What it actually did was make it easier to design.

A E   ...The tools being things like placing importance on the relationship of the threshold, a space between the front door that allows that transition from public to private realm. Or of allowing a sort of community surveillance, facilitated by having a room looking onto the street, which Georgian terraces illustrate so well. In their case those front rooms tend to be slightly elevated – so as a pedestrian you're looking up to the ceiling— but as a resident you are looking out and down on the pedestrian. You are not making eye contact because of that level change, you feel private, you feel that separation.

M H   In a funny sort of way, it's a way of adding hierarchy to all public buildings, and even private residences are public in some respects.

A E   I guess at New Islington, our spatial configuration was partly an outcome of trying to make the numbers work on a narrow site — but actually what the layout allows is for gardens to have direct relationships to the street.

M H   The site was awkward; we had an urban block that wouldn't really function with the type of units that the client wanted. But it ultimately proved to be one of the real advantages. We had one of those moments where we were messing around with this checkerboard arrangement, and thinking oh that's cute, and it meant everyone could get this and that — sunlight, a garden, on-site parking ... Suddenly we thought, if they go back-to-back, we've eliminated so much building material that we've got the budget to put into something else! The gap between units meant that semi-detached houses read as individual villas but functioned as a terrace. We really felt we'd cracked something there, it was a lovely moment.

A E   We've always wondered what the line is between creating something that is of the city and something that's individual and personal, and New Islington is perhaps a good illustration of that, too. The houses are brought together by a base of consistent brick that holds them together and gives a strong coherent building line, and then each house differs in terms of brickwork at the upper level. Over time, each dwelling has been personalised by hanging baskets, clocks and outdoor furniture — and that's the moment where you step back and life takes over the architecture. We're not so prescriptive that we don't want change to happen.

M H   I think Mæ has always in a way, and in parentheses, under-designed.

What I mean by that is that if you over-design, what you do is chase out opportunity for any sort of change, It's amazing that architects for many years have been astounded by how vulnerable a modernist façade can be to a single change — the flipside of that is to become more prescriptive. It's like Mies only having three settings for louvres: up, middle or down — but if you design something that's robust and has this…let's call it a semi-retiring characteristic, it doesn't resolve itself within itself and I think, this erosion of autonomy is an important thing for architecture. It allows for other people to come in, funnily enough it's more robust in the face of other peoples' stuff. You can read the thing more clearly somehow.

A E We're creating frameworks for people to live out their lives, you know, like a theatre of life. But that's not to say we are creating anonymity; I think it's important that our projects and anything we do maintains a strong identity.
    When I last visited Hammond Court, there was a chap sitting and working

on his balcony and neighbouring kids playing in the central garden. And it was quite satisfying to see it used in that way.

Darbourne and Darke, Marquess Estate

M H   You know, there's something about allowing tectonic concerns to step back in order to create conditions, to foster neighbourliness. Architecture which has enough presence to step back and not do the jazz-hands thing in public can be absorbed as part of a city. And that's probably why we might love pictures of Neave Brown's buildings, but why'd we prefer to live in some of Geoffrey Darke's buildings — not all of them, but some of them definitely.

Neave Brown, Alexandra Road

SB   You mentioned the word hierarchy, Michael earlier on. Can you expand on that a bit more?

MH   At different times on this island and in other places, different sorts of hierarchical tools are used to make things legible or discrete — especially with the stuff of cities. At certain points in history those hierarchies have been expressed primarily through façades, for example, neo-classical façades — we've inherited that. Sometimes that hierarchy can be established via a group of buildings; there are other urban hierarchies such as zoning. Just as we were thinking of hierarchies of individual buildings, there were other people thinking about the hierarchies of urban landscapes, but I definitely think the hierarchies of individual house-ness had been lying fallow for a while in this country. A lot of our contemporaries had started to dig back and use memory, for example looking at Georgian or Victorian terraces and how they use step-backs, half-level changes, small yards and so on — all these tools you could play with, right down to creating that sense of neighbourliness, or producing the formality of squares and crescents. And rediscovering all of this stuff felt really, like we had walked into someone else's kitchen and they had better stuff than we had and we started using it, like we were in a grown-ups kitchen as opposed to our bed-sit.

A E   It plays on the idea of drawing on what's around you. Perhaps this is the difference from the Smithsons' generation, who saw an overwhelming need to impose a singular, overarching

and original idea on neighbourhoods.
I guess we're drawing on a wider lexicon.
So in a project like Agar Grove, it's
a big estate where we are creating
a piece of city with a mix of terraces,
villas, mansion blocks and tower
blocks. We looked at Camden as
a wider neighbourhood and part of its
attractiveness is its variety.

    We're trying to use types in a meaningful way — so we've got a situation with existing Victorian villas on one side of the street and we need to respond in scale and rhythm to that, whereas there are other moments on the site where we can afford to build up, build denser and so it's appropriate to draw on other typology. The familiar forms in the area operate at an emotional level and we've sought to bring together history and type to create an architecture of the everyday.

Agar Grove, typological variety

**As-found and completed projects by Mæ architects
with photography by David Grandorge**

Agar Grove Estate   As-found

Lisson Grove   **As-found**

Tybalds Estate   **As-found**

New Islington   **Completed**

Hammond Court **Completed**

Wilbury Hills **Completed**

November 11, 2013

S B So would you say the m-house, for example, could make us rethink what constitutes a home? Let's talk about that one as an early project.

m-house

A E Well, I suppose the m-house encapsulates so much of what we are interested in as a practice. On the one hand we were interested in fabrication and we had a strong desire to make something feel domestic, despite being lightweight and mobile. And we were already interested in asking how we might work with legislation in a positive way.

M H It's a project for a client who wanted a caravan, so it was absolutely based on caravan legislation. The legislation sets a maximum size and stipulates that the structure must arrive on site in no more that two pieces; it's got to have wheels but it doesn't necessarily have to be road-worthy, things like that. We thought we could zip up a building, a dry building and a wet building — serviced and unserviced — zip them together. It was still a caravan but we designed it to be built to better standards than building regulations for a house at the time. The maximum size allowed us to create a home of 100 square metres.

m-house, interior

A E It's as big as a Hoxton loft, twice the size of a typical one-bedroom flat, and we were thinking about modern methods of construction, building and prefabricated components in factories... That was fun. We were desperately trying to consider its wider relevance for housing supply, given that land value seemed out of control in London and the south east – even at that time.

S B That was prescient – when was that, when were you thinking about land value for the m-house?

M H That was back in 2002. And we thought, we've cracked it! We've split building cost and land value so you can just put these things wherever you want...

A E It seems land ownership and law shape our cities, but we were lucky that the possibility to separate those issues was already part of this commission. m-house made us think about how one can use architecture – or how we as architects and town planners can contribute – towards solving some of those really tangible problemsin society, of the shortage in housing, affordability, where you locate...

M H The m-house would allow people to buy their home and rent the land that it sits on, rather like living on a houseboat. Of course, the intractable problem is getting mortgage lenders to think differently about where value lies.

Lift-Up House

A E It plays into broader concern of ours, how we provide different models for housing, for meeting need, for giving people choice and increasing the variety in provision of housing. m-house is one those, also Lift-Up House; though both were very specific commissions to design one-off buildings, they represent models which carry our broader thinking. So Lift-Up House is a rooftop home – one of our students worked out that a if you just added a single storey on the rooftops across London, you could appropriate something like the accommodation area of Leeds.

MH They were definitely related because the second client had seen the first project and wanted the same thing. And we realised we couldn't do that, because we couldn't give him an off-the-shelf solution.

Lift-Up House view towards City of London

A E Lift-Up House is a contemporary reinterpretation of the weaver's loft, a conspicuous type in this part of East London. It's a glazed pavilion of classical proportions sitting on a brick industrial building. It makes reference to the City of London which is visible to the south; we have drawn on the familiar corporate glass world but here we use a more mundane industrial glass and play with transparency.

S B We were talking about this last time weren't we, this variation in transparency and opacity in the city.

A E Yes, you get all this corporate glassiness to the south of our building, generic and hermetically sealed curtain walled offices. Lift-Up House is not transparent in a way that the city office building is, despite being all glass. Industrial glazing runs in front of insulated walls, and then windows are introduced into the profiled glass to frame views of the city. Translucent screens pull back for privacy or open up for aspect. The building is intended to draw peoples' attention to its social and contextual background.

M H   ...There are all these little things, individual ideas — they're like loads and loads of little projects that you put together and it makes a decent house.

A E   The point was that although they were specific briefs, specific clients, we nonetheless thought they were models or types that had a wider application. In a sense they are hypothetical, because we've not gone into business to create mobile housing or rooftop houses.

S B   This idea of typology and types seems to be a useful tool for you, when you discuss your work.

A E   Yes, it can be a means of starting a conversation.
  You might start by thinking about what kind of place are we trying to create, and as soon as you mention a type, people can form in their minds approximately the sense of scale you're trying to achieve, what the morphology might be, what the character could be, and so it is a useful starting point. But

I don't want it to hamstring us. In projects like our proposal for Chobham Manor we were exploring the gamut of type. This was our shortlisted scheme to design the extension to the Olympic Park and the brief was very much about how you design family houses in the city. So we started by questioning just what is the family today. It isn't restricted to your classical nuclear family; there are single-parent families, reconstituted families, there are vertically extended, modified nuclear, horizontally extended...

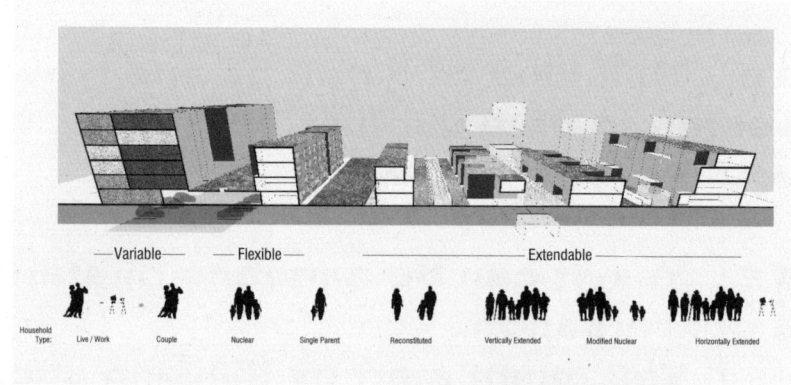

Chobham Manor, family types diagram

S B   All described in spatial terms!

A E   Exactly! But actually they are classic sociological definitions. And as a result, we were trying to think what are the types, how do you re-imagine types to accommodate those different family conditions? For example, we might look at horizontally extended family, where you have a family co-habiting with aunts or uncles, so families stay together even though they're married. Certain cultural groups will extend their households.

S B   That's how I grew up – in houses with uncles or aunts who might have been siblings but who had their own families too.

A E   So there we were thinking is that the re-invention of the terraced house? These fantastic terraces where something that looks like a single house can offer the flexibility of separate maisonettes or several flats – so that the horizontally extended family can retreat into their separate spaces or come together. Whereas accommodating what we imagined as the vertically extended family – something like the granny moving back in – lead us to thinking about a house and an associated mews house. You might want something with an annexe in the back or a studio that can give her independence but can offer support and help from the family when she needs it.

S B   A studio, too, for those people who are starting to work from home...

M H   This is one of the challenges in how we want our cities to be. Walking around in my neighbourhood for instance; there's some pretty nice council housing right in the middle of Hampstead Village, such as Wells House[1] for example...

1 Wells House, Hampstead designed by CH James in 1948, designed to harmonise with the Grade 1 listed Burgh House of 1703

Wells House, Hamsptead

S B   Do you know when it dated from?

M H   It was built just after the second war, but it's like the 1930s designs dusted off, really nice. Even when it was built, when Hampstead was probably a little less arty and rich, you've got a really nice urban juxtaposition where you have council housing within a broader social mix, and that's wonderful. It's just about big enough to see that they developed a typology. It is built effectively, for a certain amount of money – but it's not so big that it forms a ghetto. Rather it opens up and in fact junctions very well with the buildings around there.

Sometimes these larger council buildings lock in with the little streets with rows of houses, but then within buildings, the configuration might have to be flexible; one of the things that anyone who has designed housing, or is working on it, will know. A social housing client might come to you needing some kind of configuration of four or five units and they might say: We've got a Mrs Riley whose disabled and we need two studios and we need another two-bed — oh no, actually make that another studio because we've got a guy who's coming out of prison next week... Suddenly, you've got this building where it seems that you have to design a game of Tetris.

A E   Exactly.

M H   And you can do that, that's great, and the client thinks so too. But what happens once you've knocked your pipe to do this, somehow keeping a coherent urban approach and then the clients say, can we just turn that unit into a three-bedroom? There's a big question, one that comes up again and again. If you're too specific in architecture, then what you do is lock things, and urbanistically being too specific can create monocultures. That, we believe, is not a good thing — going back to thinking about type — the task is to design plasticity and flexibility inside the buildings.
  The best kind of flexibility really is a geezer with a hammer and his mate, carting the crap out of the door... that's how you get flexibility! In a way our choice about the means of construction

determines the possibilities for change, working within party walls or not, being conservative or pushing things around.

A E   I guess Chobham Manor expresses a number of approaches to flexibility. In fact we talk about variable, flexible and extendable as separate things, to try and differentiate between, for example, the thing you're describing with party walls, which would fall within the flexible definition. When you're building terraces with traditional construction, then yes, you have stay on the party walls but you can move partitions around. But if you're building an apartment block with a concrete frame, as Hammond Court was, it's irrelevant: all you need to do is stack the soil pipes. This allows even more variability about the mix of accommodation that you can fit with in the frame, the party walls between flats can move. It's sort of like Maison Domino versus Mæ's Party Wall project.

S B   So you would describe Hammond Court as allowing variability as opposed to the fixed terrace?

M H   Absolutely, and that's the key isn't it...

A E   We wanted to create a building with a coherent urban identity but we had this Tetris-like arrangement of flats and maisonettes. By planning to a module—for example, a 5.5×9 metre grid—it gave us the optimum structural shell to alternatively accommodate a couple of two bedrooms flats either side of a core or a one bedroom and a three bedroom, or combine two stacked one bedrooms to create a family maisonette.

Hammond Court, arrangement of dwelling mix

S B   If a unit became available next to you would you be able to extend, like plot-landers? Technically that should be possible, right, if you're just working on a frame?

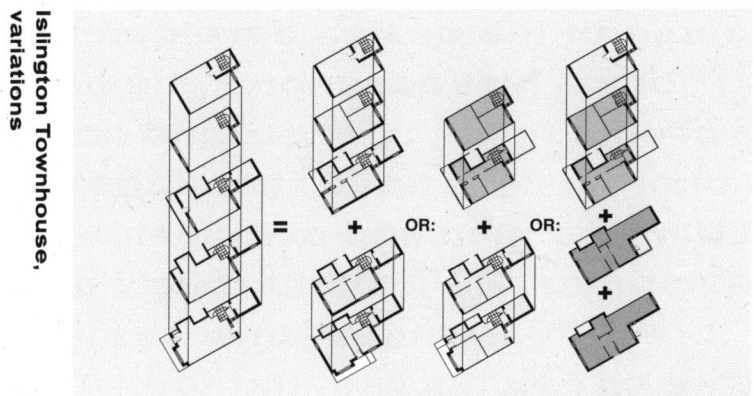
Islington Townhouse, variations

A E   Yeah, I guess so. Another approach is illustrated in our competition entry for the Islington Townhouse. Here, the outrigger – an outrigger with floors at half-landings that we add to the rear – becomes a really important spatial device, because it can belong to the flat above or below, offering more space to whichever dwelling needs it. So you can combine a three bed or a maisonette, or maisonette above a family house or as needs change, you could even negotiate to buy the spare room on the landing off the flat above if they've downsized.

I think that's the ideal, that one is producing a house that can develop to

meet their changing needs, but it's also the fact — as in this case of Hammond Court — that the market can change over the course of the design development. Or as Michael just described, the needs of the clients might change, and can often change right up to the stage of submitting for planning permission.
So we need to design generously and allow loose-fit arrangements. In many ways the city works like that too.

November 27, 2013

S B   We've talked a few times about weaving together parts of London that belong to different times, and the sensitivity needed to do that. In fact, we've used lots of metaphors, from stitching to dental surgery. Can we talk about how your projects fit into the pre-existing fabric of the city?

A E   The project that has recently focused my mind on this idea of retrospective integration – is that too much like jargon? – is the Tybalds Estate in Holborn. We explored how, through new interventions, we might knit and stitch together different bits of history. The site we're dealing with is really rich in its history. We have Great Ormond Street and Lamb's Conduit Street, with those beautiful Victorian and Georgian terraces; against that, you've got a couple of 1950s slab blocks. Both are ideals of their time, models of what good housing could be. Steen Eiler Rasmussen talks about those terraces of Bloomsbury being the sort of epitome of thoughtful, good housing.

M H   It's a sort of restrained urbanism.

Tybalds housing estate model

A E You've also got two 1960s tower blocks, built on the location of back to back terrace houses that have been cleared out or possibly even bomb damaged. So you've got at least three generations or at least three very different urban conditions and periods of housing. We've been looking to do a bit of dental surgery, a bit of stitching in that holds them all together.

There was a master plan that we were given as a brief, which showed a new terrace fronting onto the existing terrace which we instinctively felt was the wrong answer.

S B   What was the wrong answer?

A E   Putting a new terrace opposite the existing terrace; it's not so much that we don't kind of believe in that condition, creating a good street with housing on both sides – but actually what it did is it turned its back on the 1970s tower blocks. We felt that they needed to be acknowledged, in exactly the same way anything Georgian or Victorian or something that is slightly more prized would be.

In the case of Tybalds, actually, the two towers are fine: they're perfectly popular and make good housing. The problem is that they don't relate to their context; they're sort of alien and there's an opportunity – and this is the point – to retrospectively integrate them into a streetscape that works.

M H   It's interesting that tower blocks seem to offend people. We were talking before about the concern of looking up the skirt of Victoria and instinctively needing to have something like a plinth around there, to hide her ankles. I think generally what we do is we build up to them; but there is potential of enormous drama and public space adjacent to the base of large towers, once you have defined territories.

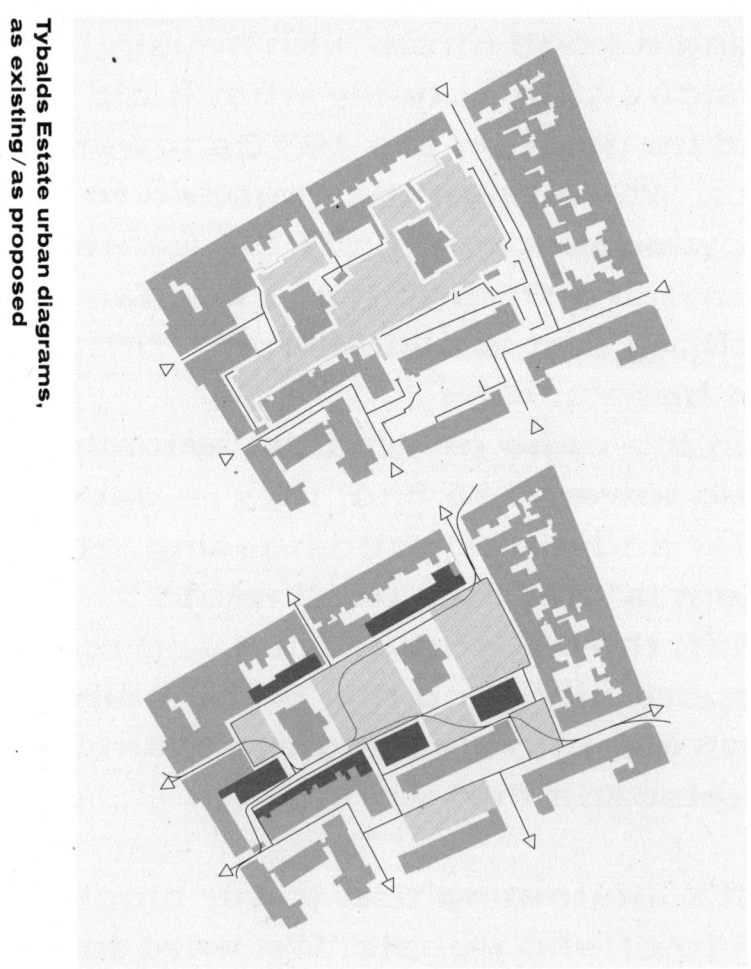

Tybalds Estate urban diagrams, as existing / as proposed

A E   That is exactly the approach we've taken; the intention was to give greater definition to what we have, rather than trying to recreate a sort of

Victorian street that ignores the whole post-war history in the middle.

M H   That ignores the 'problem', meaning the tower.

A E   Exactly. We managed to get the number of houses that we needed elsewhere on the site. I think what we've really tried to do here is give meaning back to those two towers, as well as bringing the existing terrace into that conversation. We have inserted one row of mews houses, against the back of the garden walls of the Great Ormond Street terrace, creating a new street frontage. On the other side, we've got a row of maisonettes and flats, which again creates street frontage – suddenly, these two towers are now brought into a conversation with the street, instead of just sitting in an island with backs of buildings to them.
So we're creating a framed space, with a common treatment of the public realm space to give it coherence – the public space holds it all together.
   It got us thinking about the fact that a good proportion of built experiments

over time have been demolished, following a desperate feeling that we've got to clear out that stuff that didn't work – where as actually there is a real opportunity. We're doing it at Agar Grove as well, where we're retaining the 1960s tower rather on the site and refurbishing it. Again, we're putting it back into a streetscape that hopefully will allow it to work better.

Agar Grove

S B   Who's the client for Tybalds?

A E   That's the London Borough of Camden, as is Agar Grove. I think local authorities are in that great role where they can enable this sort of integration to happen. Camden's got an amazing legacy of Sydney Cook housing, the old Benson & Forsyth stuff; they did some extraordinary schemes. I think Camden, as well as some of the other local authorities we're working with, have the keeness to do high quality work. More importantly, they've got an opportunity that a commercial developer wouldn't have, because they own all those fragmented bits of land that can suddenly be brought into a conversation with each other; the red boundary line can be redrawn.

Branch Hill Estate, Camden, London, Benson and Forsyth

M H This is very different context – but if you think about the way in which rationalist, fascist-era architecture found itself a place in the older Italian cities – places like Milan and elsewhere in northern Italy – even Mussolini didn't believe he could demolish too much historical fabric. Through critical discourse, their architects found a way to work with existing stuff; they were very often looking for opportunities that might have been left behind from the Quarto Cento. As we walk through our cities, we recognise opportunities, weaknesses and problems; there are probably innumerable 'given the opportunity' pub conversations, which point to potential sites on local authority owned land right now in London. I think there is something about that stuff, the retrospective stuff, that compels you to think, 'Someone just retrofit that city!'

A E Well, the nature of architecture has changed. Our role today is about developing a collective vision bringing together investors, planners, public and users. The opportunities are significant, all over London. With something like Tybalds, while it doesn't share the grandeur of the Barbican scheme or the tabula rasa of modernist estates, it has a scale that is still significant. There are three built interventions holding a place together, and in addition there are extensions and overbuilds. In total we're adding 93 homes in a very small, central area of London; this coherence and cumulative value is what pushes the scheme beyond being a sort of interstitial infill project, to be greater than the sum of its parts.

Nordhavnen

I suppose we did explore big vision place making in our proposal for Nordhavnen. That was fun; if you are given a site of 400 hectares, what do you do with it? In that case we proposed two district centres, three neighbourhood centres and a series of character areas. We used built form to create coherence and give legibility to the centre, but then allowed for a fragmentation around the edges, as density falls away.

MH Maybe this is exactly the strength of our generation – we do in fact work with conglomerate architecture and we don't think in terms of the 'total' or overarching vision of the thing. We think in terms of the moment, of conversations like 'You know how you walk into that square in Holborn and then there's that bit there.' All these moments are whimsical in nature, really.

AE Which is how you experience the city.

MH It's probably one of the things that Mæ has always felt. And possibly a characterisation of our generation is that whimsy, or a kind of whimsical enjoyment of city, of the ineffable bits of architecture. We can't help but do it because we, as a generation, have learned to navigate cities over and again, whether we've grown up through the changes of London or moved around elsewhere. There's something about the history of the people involved in making those decisions in terms of architecture and planning, which is a new thing; they are in fact more literate about how bits of the city work – and especially bits that don't work that well – because that's where they've had to live. Therefore you don't get a Corbusian response to something, because people have had to make their way around it.

A E   I don't shy away from developing big ideas; that's the reason we did Nordhavnen, because we want to make pieces of city and we've got ideas that can contribute to how cities should be built. But they are not ideas that promote a single solution, like Villa Radieuse.

S B   It seems strange now to imagine something so self-contained. At least, here.

A E   Yes, it doesn't engage with the world as it exists. I guess we're trying to marry up big strategic thinking with places as we find them. So in Nordhavnen, it was about how we can develop a city around the Enlightenment ideal of a grid whilst creating places that have variety and diversity, recognising what happens at the scale of the human and the street.

M H   Again, I think that is a product of a sort of urban immersion. It's no accident that London could set up a bike riding scheme now. It wouldn't have been possible twenty or even ten years ago — there weren't enough riders. There's a re-engagement with the urban condition — the opposite of white flight, it's the middle class coming back into town. This is an interesting historical time and I think this architecture is a product of it; it doesn't seek to turn from the city as suburbs do, as perhaps even the Barbican does; inside, it's great but it makes a suburb in a town, it is essentially suburban in its will. Instead what we're getting is an architecture that turns to the city and that makes an attempt to be neighbourly. London is an immigrant town, immigrants from different social groups, internal as well as international immigration. The thing about post-rational urban integration is that it runs hand in hand with the diversity of our society – which is extraordinary. We could either have whole neighbourhoods that are ghetto-ised or we could have a city, which is massively diverse.

Barbican Estate, City of London, Chamberlin Powell and Bon

S B   There's probably a relationship between that diversity, and a cynicism or a resistance to grands projets… you mentioned the Smithsons, but their 'ideal nuclear unit' or the Corbusian 'cell', is no longer seen as universal or indeed necessarily 'ideal'.

Tybalds Estate, courtyard houses

A E   With Tybalds, the mix of type and scale is an outcome of our observations on site and of the site's fragmented character. So the courtyard houses are going to be very large, for affluent buyers – but are by necessity houses, because we couldn't fit anything else in the space; they're limited by the height of the garden wall they sit against. On the other side of the street are the more affordable terrace houses and shared ownership flats. In Chobham Manor, there is not much of an architectural context to draw from so diversity comes from questioning the family-oriented brief. However, we still try to create coherence, as at New Islington, or in the identity of the housing at Hammond Court whilst creating housing that can accommodate that sheer variety.

M H   As well as encouraging an architectural fecundity, it is important to value what is already in the city. Not the big vision thing, but rather a sort of urban gardening that allows people to value what's around them, what parts of this culture already have value inherently. In a way our training makes us read buildings and urban conditions as a kind of school room, and citizens without formal training also value what they recognise. So enhancing, repeating and learning from existing conditions allows people to feel familiar and I think that that is one of the most important jobs of architecture and urbanism.

Identity

Sitting on the terrace of the Tate Modern, looking over the north bank of the Thames you'd be forgiven for thinking that you should be afforded one of the best views of the capital's skyline.

London's skyline

The apparent coherence of London when viewed from the sky or the general consistency of building height when standing in a typical London street is undermined when confronted with a long view across the Thames. London's skyline is varied, an incoherent jumble of competing forms and heights. Compared to central Paris's unified parapet height, or the soaring grandeur of Manhattan, London's skyline resembles nothing so much as the mouth of a gap-toothed hag with seemingly idiotic lumps of developed and under developed cityscape.

This unsatisfactory mess is no accident. The London Plan contains a number of sections rightly devoted to the protection of City monuments, the most influential, from the point of view of London's skyline being the Strategic Viewing Corridors to St. Paul's Cathedral. For those not familiar with this particular planning wease, which was penned between World War I and World War II, it sets out various protected viewing corridors usually from Royal Parks, through the City to St. Paul's. Within these corridors, buildings over certain heights are not to be generally permitted.

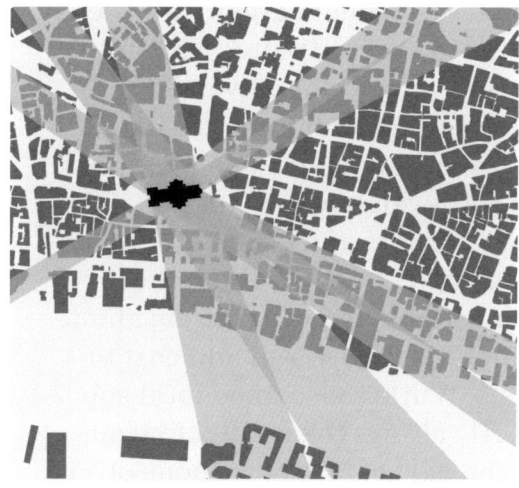

Strategic Viewing Corridors to St. Paul's Cathedral

The object at the time was presumably to unify the fast sprawling Metroland of Greater London, giving the oiks in the suburbs a view of Wren's great building. These glimpses of local, historical "high culture" would, it was hoped, galvanise Londoners in the aftermath of the socially disruptive mess of the Somme—nudging them towards

133   Identity

a resumption of their pre-war, hat-doffing lives, without recourse to the new social models of mechanistic American commercialism or the internationalist aspirations of Soviet style Communism. London's existing skyline would be rigorously policed, her institutions would remain unchanged and the Empire would be safe. Back on the terrace it seemed to us that the plan had failed; rather than unifying the City it seems to have cut it into disorientating lumps and stumps. One can see were the action is at in the average American town for miles around, as the dense downtown is taller than the suburbs. In Paris, one can orientate oneself using the axial boulevards which link institutions of power and culture. London, by contrast, has grown as a series of fragments, each distorted from the next as they change to meet the demands of private speculation and working around the constraints of planning legislation.

A crude calculation indicates that if three stories were added to the building stock constrained by these viewing corridors, the enclosed area would equal that of Leeds. Whatever the precise figure, the principle remains that this creaky planning diagram generates a lot of wasted commercial and residential potential. This creates an incoherence out of kilter with successful place-making and the formation of a city with a strong urban identity. If this situation is planned, perhaps now would be a good time to ask the question "Why do we need planning legislation at all?" The Architect's Legal Handbook says that the Town and Country Planning Act was brought about "for the simple reason that in England and Wales there is a limited amount of land for an increasing number of people who wish to live and work upon it…thus the pressure on a limited acreage of land is great and getting greater." This argument seems compelling until one considers that only 11.4% of the country is currently developed.

Most architects, especially small practitioners and especially small practitioners given a drink or two, will happily bang on about the perceived idiocies of their local planning department, whining about delays and eccentric requirements which slow work and add cost to perfectly reasonable building proposals. While these anecdotal sob stories are legion, they are not necessarily always the result of incompetence or architectural ignorance on the part of planners themselves. The problem seems systemic, given that so many planners seem to prefer buildings that were erected prior to the Act of 1947, at a time with little or no planning legislation and therefore no planning officers.

This island's developer-led planning system, in which you tell them what you would like to build and they see if they like it or not, forces planners into the reactive position of development control. There seems to be little, "planning", a word implying forethought, involved. As one might expect the unfortunate byproducts of this case by case situation are conservative decision making, muddled thinking; because of the number of local area restrictions and delay resulting from the volume of required planning applications submitted.

The current boom in individual householder development (72% of planning decisions in 2002), and our government's efforts to address the shortage of affordable housing in many of our major cities, ensures that over-worked planning departments will have less time to inspect an increasing volume of applications in future. It is hardly surprising that design agencies[1] have been rushing reports about the easing of planning restrictions to areas such as the rear of domestic buildings, where they are perceived to have little impact on the public realm; and national planning legislation has followed suit.

1   CABE, Commission for Architecture and the Built Environment and RIBA for example

Given the current incoherent system, which translates into incoherent places, perhaps it is time we stopped fiddling around with "planning" and got ourselves a simple workable "plan". Perhaps in the interest of quality cities, we remove the bureaucracy in favour of strategy-led masterplans that consider first and foremost what we want the image of the city to be in terms of structure, identity and meaning.

What would such a plan look like and what kind of outcome would it lead to? The idea of the city is conventionally founded on the principles of centre, enclosure and boundaries. Fixed form-function allows identity and coherence, but it is difficult to change and we are more drawn to open structures, which we consider more sustainable for their ability to accommodate adaptation and progress without sprawl. Cities that allow migration, growth and change stimulate cultural development. In this context we advocate strategy led masterplanning rather than deterministic and fixed models: open versus closed system. Our approach would adopt the following principles:

* Prioritise public realm as a space of difference and democracy.
* Facilitate mutualism i.e neighbouring buildings derive benefit without being fully dependant
* Build structures capable of adaptation and change
* Treat edges as seams—the threshold to the house, the stoa at the edge of the square, the facade of a building—become mediating devices for environmental or social exchange.
* Derive environmental benefit and minimise consumption
* Promote mixed use to encourage diversity and sustain future patterns of inhabitation.

Is this approach compatible with creating identity? Without the constraints of the viewing corridors, the city would be allowed to grow and intensify in a way that would lend temporal coherence until societal change offers new direction. Towers would naturally cluster much as members of tribes gather together. Houses and buildings could be extended in ways that enhance their local context. Fragmented zones characterised by singular land use would become a seamlessly connected part of the continuity of the city, while hermetic, speculative built forms would be replaced by enabling structures that engage with the climate and society around.

The State

The influence of the State on architecture has long been of interest to Mæ. Whilst good architecture must be generated by ideas beyond the practical and the technical we nonetheless recognise that there is a role for legislation when speculation and the liberty of the market work against the interests of the common good. Architects have a duty to influence the legislator, bringing as they do a perspective on what makes successful buildings and places, on the history of architecture and the demands of our time.

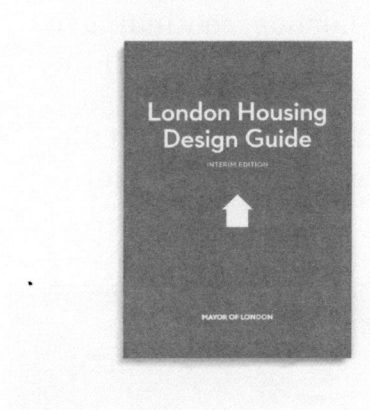

London Housing Design Guide

Our responsibility is both to our client and to those who visit, pass by and occupy our buildings. We consider the needs of citizens and can consequently be proactive in shaping the very forces that shape our buildings.

The Mayor of London's London Housing Design Guide and subsequent London Planning Guidance introduces mandatory requirements for all housing developments in Greater London. The development of the Design Guide with the London Development Agency was an absorbing commission for Mæ, and generated lively debate regarding its proposals.

The Design Guide covers areas such as appropriate housing density, street proportion, dwelling space standards and circulation design. Its recommendations were arrived at as a result of a synthetic approach to the plethora of existing guidance. The Design Guide cuts existing documents governing London housing design down to a fifth of their previous number, making life easier for everyone involved with the procurement, design and construction of housing.

Superseded documents include:
* Housing Quality Indicators
* Lifetime Homes
* Building for Life
* Secured By Design

Our appointment to develop the new guidance offered us an opportunity to refine our thoughts on the nature and anatomy of good domestic architecture. We have noticed a tendency among younger, predominantly London-based architectural practices to develop housing typologies based on familiar and culturally legible models. The Mayor of London talks about the development of a "New Vernacular for London Housing". If we understand him correctly, this can be assisted by guidance based on a sound understanding of London's best architectural precedents as well as a realistic approach to the social and economic forces at work in our city today. London has a long history of enacting forward thinking housing guidance. The most successful, we would argue, were the Building Acts developed immediately after the Great Fire of London, continuing to the middle of the nineteenth century. The Acts were the first building control legislation to be adopted, with minor variation, throughout Britain. Perhaps this precedent suggests that the introduction of the Design Guide should be of more than passing interest to other metropolitan authorities.

The Great Fire of London, etching

One of the strengths of the Acts resided in their ability to galvanise political will behind the revision of permissible building forms and techniques immediately after the fire. It should be remembered that this was in the face of strong resistance from large sections of the capital's business community, who saw the introduction of fireproof construction as a ruinous extravagance.

While the aesthetic implications of load-bearing brick façades and fire-separating party walls might not have been immediately apparent to the casual observer, Londoners of the period could not have missed the removal of overhanging timber eves, cornices and other complex projecting building elements in favour of brick or stone parapets and façades. The setback of other timber components, such as windows and doors, added to a clean and ordered architectural effect in harmony with the aesthetic disciplines of Palladian and then neoclassical taste. The symbiotic role the Acts played in the development of London's restrained and refined Georgian architecture is perhaps their most profound legacy.

The Acts also set ratios for road width and defined the size of buildings intended to line them, in terms of the building's rateable value based on size and ground rent. The number of these rated types might appear a little limited—only four dwelling sizes were defined—however this perhaps reveals the city fathers' intention to create a handsome uniformity for streets of the New Jerusalem.

The consistency of plan exhibited by terraces of this period remained basically unchanged into the late nineteenth century, when accumulated alterations in domestic habit required different forms. Hermann Muthesius noted in his book Das Englische Haus (1904-5), the development of a peculiarly British domestic architecture based upon a profound self-awareness of what makes a home. The example of Gallop's Homestead by C.H.B. Quennell, presents the ur-British suburban plan; anyone living in an inter-war semi will know its comforts well.

Muthesius noted a similarity in domestic requirements across social class and income groups, give or take the number of rooms in a dwelling. It was perhaps this unity of understanding, added to commitments made by His Majesty's Government to improve working class housing during World War I, which led to the first governmental housing space standards. Prior to the Tudor Walters report of 1918, model by-laws had little to say on

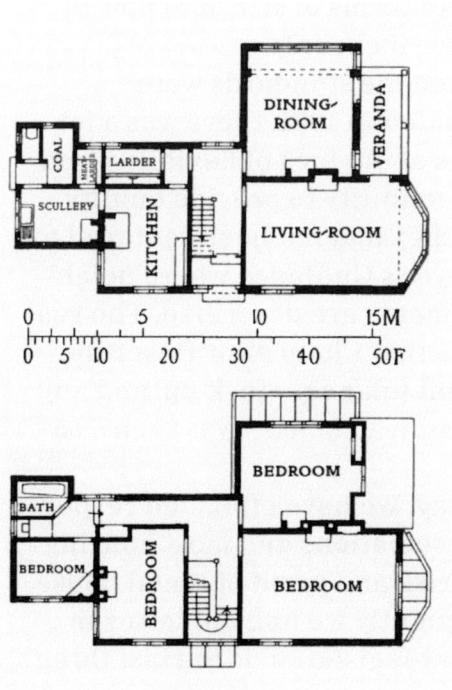

Gallop's Homestead, C.H.B Quennell

The State

the subject of dwelling size. House builders largely ignored standards developed by charitable organs, because the working classes could not generally afford to buy their products.

Space standards for the first local authority housing tended to be lower than their private equivalent. By the 1930s, however, the effects of the depression on the British housing market had caused the relationship to flip. The disparity between public and private housing size has continued almost continuously since. It seems to be a peculiarly British phenomenon: on the continent, public housing is usually always smaller than its private equivalent.

It is interesting to note that this disparity was at its lowest during the late 1960s and early 1970s, following the publication of the Parker Morris standards in 1961 (published as Homes for today & tomorrow). A period of standards stability was ushered in following their becoming mandatory some six years later, which allowed all sectors of the construction industry to become familiar with their requirements, fostering broad agreement on what an acceptable house might be; at least in terms of size, and how to achieve it cheaply.

Parker Morris report, Homes for today & tomorrow

When the standards were rescinded in 1981, there was a lot of talk about lack of flexibility and their inability to provide quality estates design. However this is an area they had not been required to address in the first place, unlike the Mayor's Guidance where neighbourhood, density and amenity requirements are described. The real reason for rescinding Parker Morris was that Chancellor Heseltine was having problems making government finances stack-up, and any reduction in the number and size of subsidised houses was seen as a good thing.

This brings us nicely to the present day. We have offloaded responsibility for public housing to housing associations and most housing associations have in turn offloaded the risk and profit of social house building to private developers—consequently we find ourselves in a bit of a pickle. Some will argue that new legislation is the last thing that we need when the property market is stagnant, when prices have fallen and when we still have problems with affordability. But new homes in London have some of the smallest rooms in Europe with an average size of a newly built home of only 76 square metres, compared with 109 square metres in Germany and 88 square metres in Ireland. House builders find themselves unable to shift surplus, un-sellable stock onto housing associations because their design and build quality just isn't good enough to meet government funding requirements. The Government's design agency[1] recently reported that less than 20% of recent developments in London were rated good or very good.

Relaxing performance and environmental standards for housing now would only serve short-term interests. Rather like our banking industry, the business model of house builders needs to change. Land speculation and quick return for shareholders as opposed to home building and long term investment has only served to reduce the quality of housing for all sectors.

We suggest that the present construction hiatus is the perfect time to develop improved housing solutions for the future. Rather than damage commercial viability, the Mayor's Guidance is an effective way of assisting the industry to produce housing that people genuinely want to live in.

The question then arises as to whether such standards can apply nationally. If the Mayor of London's housing standards — specifically the space standards — were applied nationally, it could be seen to exacerbate an already intrusive and regulation-rich climate in Britain, which restricts freedoms and discourages individual responsibility. However, such parity could also improve tranparency, amenity and encourage a fairer society, where everyone has a right to a reasonable amount of space to dwell.

These are the sorts of question that ministers face when considering their responsibilities for dealing with perceived problems in society. We have been working as part of an independent group of building industry experts, tasked with simplifying the mass of rules imposed on developers and house builders. One area for analysis is the need or otherwise for space standards.

As architects who design housing we would welcome less red tape, fewer rules and regulations. The aforementioned Lifetime Homes, the Code for Sustainable Homes, Secured by Design, Housing Quality Indicators along with British Standards, Building Bulletins, Planning Policy Guidance Notes and the fourteen parts of the Building Regulations are still applied nationally and could all do with a good pruning. The London Housing Design Guide offers a model of how this can be done, allowing architects to side-step all of the above, with the exception of Building Regulations. The space standards in the London

	Kitchen	Dining	Living	Combined Kitchen/ Living/Dining:	Double	Twin	Single	Storage/Utility	Bathroom	additional WC
baseline				add 21 sq.m + 2 sq.m p/p	add 12 sq.m	add 12 sq.m	add 8 sq.m	add 1 sq.m + 0.5 sq.m p/p	add 4.4 sq.m	2.7 sq.m
studio										
1-person				21 sq.m			8 sq.m	1 sq.m		2.7+0.3* sq.m
1-bedroom										
2-persons				23 sq.m	12 sq.m			1.5 sq.m	4.4 sq.m	
2-bedroom										
3-persons				25 sq.m	12 sq.m		8 sq.m	2 sq.m	4.4 sq.m	2.7 sq.m
2-bedroom										
4-persons				27 sq.m	12 sq.m	12 sq.m		2.5 sq.m	4.4 sq.m	2.7 sq.m
3-bedroom										
5-persons				29 sq.m	12 sq.m	12 sq.m	8 sq.m	3 sq.m	4.4 sq.m	2.7 sq.m
4-bedroom										
6-persons				31 sq.m	12 sq.m	12 sq.m	8 sq.m + 8sq.m	3.5 sq.m	4.4 sq.m	2.7 sq.m

London Housing Design Guide, space standards matrix

Housing Design Guide proved most controversial, but I would argue that they represent the most civilising and socially just component of the Mayor's requirements.

The need to measure and manage what is fair, the need to survey, to define boundaries within which to occupy, has long been a basis for making cities. Yet we seem to have little consensus that there should be a fair and reasonable minimum amount of space in which to dwell.

The Land Ordinance Grid of 1785 was devised by Thomas Jefferson as a model for surveying, partitioning and distributing land in the United States. It became the instrument for the division of land proposing the use of a grid of varying dimensions. It determined the distribution and density of townships with the ambition to be egalitarian and democratic. It had a universal applicability regardless of topography or geology. The London Housing Design Guide's space standards have an egalitarian ambition to define a measure for

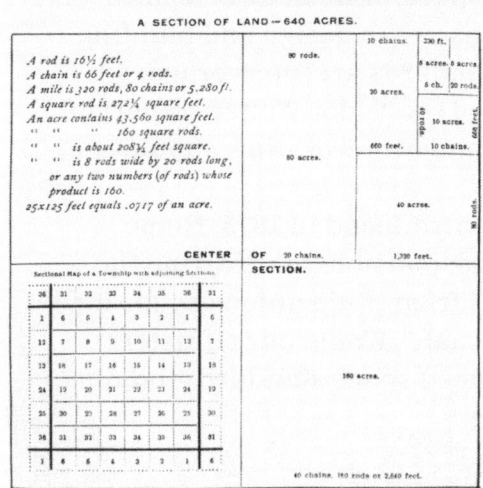

Thomas Jefferson's Land Ordinance Grid

a home deemed the minimum for a certain level of occupancy.

The industry carps on about the impact space standards will have on viability and affordability. 'We can't introduce national housing standards such as space because it will stop the delivery of housing' they say. 'We can't extend the London Housing Design Guide Standards outside London because viability is different in Middlesborough compared with Mayfair'. Well, house building has already stopped nationwide and nobody can blame this on the fact that we now have to spend a bit more insulating new homes or putting a WC on the ground floor. I have not heard anyone say that the width required for streets today affects viability—so we should repeal the London Building Act of 1667, or leave the decision to include drainage to the market, erasing the Public Health Act 1875? If such provisions seemed essential historically, why then do we find it socially acceptable to continue building the smallest houses in Europe?

Viability is what we choose it to be and regulation is collectively made in the interests of creating a civilised society. If we want things to be cheap then we can expect poor quality and in the case of housing, we can expect the knock-on consequences of poor space standards—overcrowding, poor health, poor accessibility, stress and anxiety, family tension and lack of privacy.

Some architects engaged in a profession known for its social tendencies, argue that choice about the amount of space should be a matter for the consumer—all will be rosy if we simply declare how big a home is. This suggests that cultural advancement is no longer a matter for architects—that we should merely respond to, and act as brokers within, an unfair market.

Whilst for those who argue that spatial minima constrains our creativity or is an affront to a designer's ability, I would suggest that we perhaps focus our design efforts on how we might build more for less. As Rem Koolhaas observed in his manifesto Delirious New York, the constraints of Manhattan's two-dimensional grid creates unprecedented freedom for three-dimensional anarchy, creating a metropolis of rigid chaos, could it not be the same for a home?

Well-planned, generously lit and spacious homes are as important in delivering sustainability as urban design and building performance. The fact that space standards are, on average, back to where they were at the time of the Tudor Walters report of 1918, introduced to deal with slums and overcrowding, should give us cause for concern.

When the Public Health Act was introduced in 1875, Home Secretary Richard Cross, who was responsible for drafting the legislation, received much good will from trade union groups for "humanising the toil of the working man". Would our ministers receive such plaudits if they introduced space standards today?

Society

As architects, we operate in a privileged world of being able to shape the world around us. How we shape it will depend on how we mediate between circumstances, ideas and ambitions. This need not be an ambition in the sense of modernism's heroic agenda, rather a more humane ambition that has an ethical dimension, building on social responsibility. As well as finite buildings and set pieces, architects can create flexible frameworks capable of change and strategies for customisation, acting as an enabling force to help society better meet its goals.

Custom-build opportunities in the UK tend to be limited to individuals working on marginal and suburban sites, yet it is a form of housing provision that operates outside the world of speculation, responding instead to actual and identifiable needs. We at Mæ have been exploring what the barriers are and the potential is for large scale self-build in an urban setting and what role there might be for the architect to create a better framework, which can enable custom-build housing.

The custom-build market is a valuable but often overlooked provider of housing in the UK. Self-build and self-procured projects, which we are collectively calling custom build, currently make up approximately 10–12% of new housing in the UK. This means that the output of the custom build sector is higher or at least comparable to the output of the largest single volume house builder in this country.

However, this is piffling compared with say Germany, where the self-procured sector can take up as much as 55% of the total new housing market, or France where it hovers at around the 45% mark. We believe that the market in the UK for self-build, co-operative, catalogue/kit and self-procured housing is so much greater then at present.

The Joseph Rowntree Foundation anticipates that the custom build sector could reach 20,000 units per annum. A survey by Norwich and Peterborough Building Society revealed that 70% of current homeowners have considered the idea of building their own homes—that is just the people already on the housing ladder, never mind those who rent or find themselves without a permanent home right now. Over 100,000 homeless households are living in temporary accommodation. This figure is the highest on record and increasing year on year.

One of the problems for this sector is that of density. Most kit-homes are essentially suburban in outlook, and plot costs for individuals in city settings are often prohibitively expensive. Our wonderful "timbery Scandinavian world[1]" gets a bit complex in terms of fire spread when we get closer than one metre to the party boundary.

This boundary is, we believe, a key to pull individual family

¹ Referring to prefabricated timber houses such as Scandiahus or Svenskhomes

self-builders into town. As with barrier rails on stairs in the circulation spaces of large sports venues (four people can use a three metre wide stairway if it has a central barrier rail, as opposed to just two people without), the party wall acts as a cleavage—simultaneously separating and bringing together.

The Party Wall project, developed by Mæ, aims to enable the self procurement of housing by providing the infrastructure that can help deliver custom build housing at a density required today, achieving economies of scale through the efficient use of land.

It is a system of serviced plots and, as its name suggests, party walls. First of all, footings are installed below ground to hold a load-bearing façade and party wall structure. All service connections are brought to the plot and capped off at screed level. The party walls are structurally and acoustically separated, if next door takes a year to complete their house and you have finished in three months you do not want to be bothered on Saturday morning by their power tools etc. The walls provide all the structure for a project, which is designed to accommodate simple sawn timber joist floor decks. The parameters for detailed design such as materials could be agreed across the whole self-build neighbourhood with the Local Authority and could be subject to an agreed set of design codes to give some certainty of outcome, if a degree of consistensy is felt to be a priority.

So we know who these potential custom-builders are: they would seem to be most of us. But why do people want to build their own home in the first place? Cost benefits are often cited as the reason for embarking upon this route of procurement, however because custom build sector is so small in this country, and because the sites are often single plot or with only a few units, there may not be the economies of scale which any volume house builder can pass on, even with their 10–15% profit margin.

Crucially, co-operative custom-build housing schemes offer benefits in terms of establishing social capital early on in the development of a project; they offer educational benefits, evidenced through a number of enabled self-build training programs run by housing associations. The enabled group approach to self-procured housing provision offers the potential to create a truly sustainable community. The clients or customers of this sector tend to get the homes they want, rather than what they are offered. But as well as product satisfaction, perhaps the greatest payback for this sector would seem at a neighbourhood level. If custom build is enabled at a large scale it offers the chance to hothouse communities.

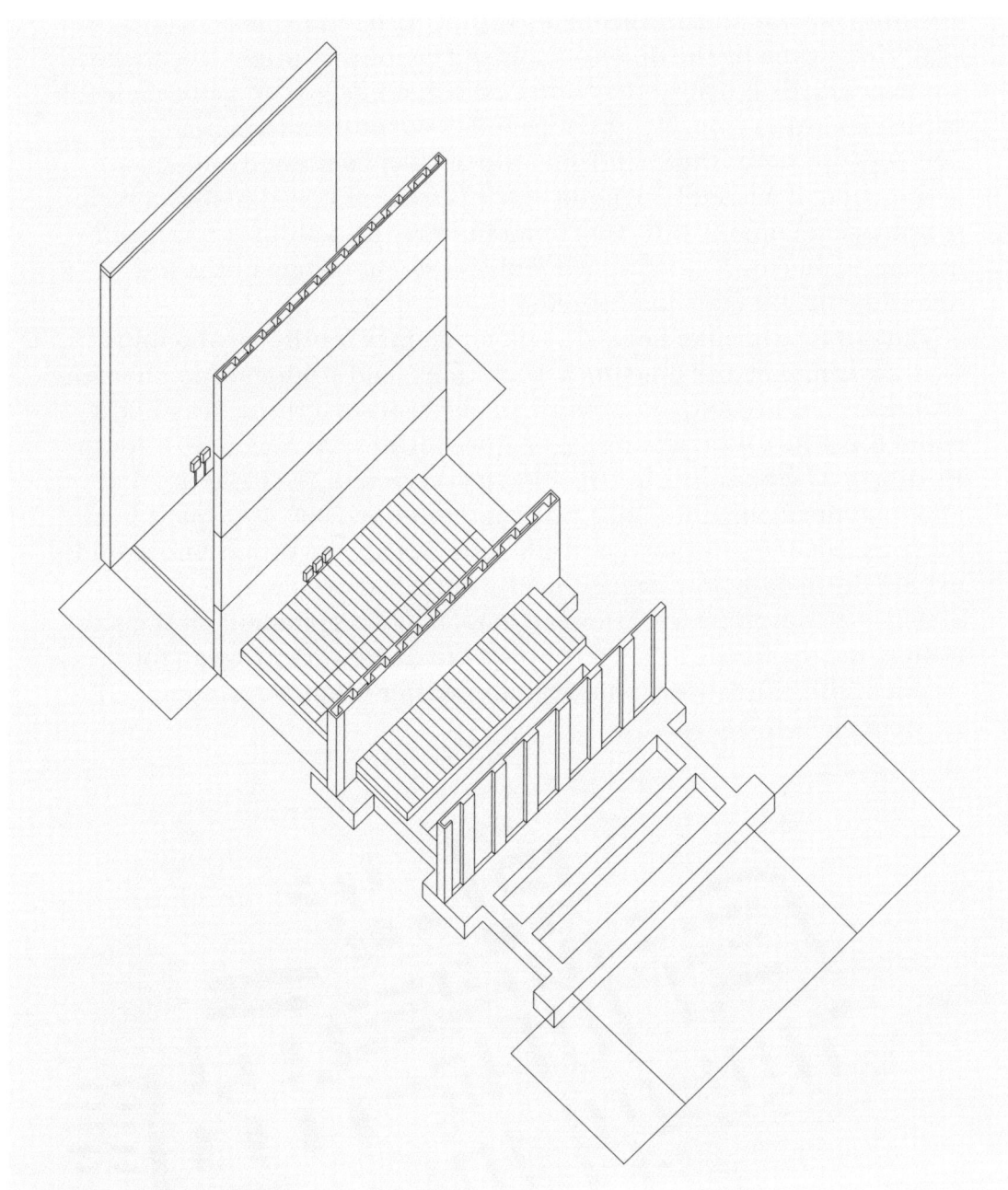

Party Wall project, axonometric

If you or your next-door neighbour or the chap up the road not only built all the houses in your street, but also the bin-store, or planted the trees in the pavement outside, the sense of community ownership is enormous. Building together means that those involved would get the chance to know each other. Many people in London, in recent years, have watched disaffectedly as well-meaning, well-designed, well-built social housing schemes rapidly eroded in short order, sometimes even by the disenfranchised youth who might live there—not necessarily because they don't care, but because it is not their job to pick up after them. Neighbourhoods take quite a long time to develop—perhaps the social speed-dating of combined endeavour is required, if a neighbourhood spirit is to be fostered before a widespread social apathy kills the 'hood in vitro. It's not just an issue of getting a "nice new neighbourhood"—it might be one of the few ways to build a neighbourhood full-stop.

Vauban is a German housing development were the local population, government and housing associations, and student union housing organisations appear, in our view, to have got something drastically right. It is a new district on a 38 hectare former barrack site in south Freiburg. The planning for the district started in 1993, the third and final development phase was completed in 2006. It forms a home for some 5000 inhabitants, and 600 jobs. It's all the things one would expect these days: low energy, pretty much car-free and dense, which is achieved by not allowing detached development on the site, though not too dense as a maximum four stories are allowed for each building and priority is given to smaller group development, i.e. no strip block nonsense.

Vauban, figure ground plan

What is interesting about this scheme is the manner in which the local city authority (which happens to be the site owner), sought to create a socially diverse city district in a participatory manner, enabling individuals and groups to procure their own homes. The initial stages of the development consisted of an urban design competition for a masterplan and implementation strategy. A group of local citizens formed an organisation called Forum Vauban. They were recognised and financially supported by the city of Freiburg as a legal body forming a sort of client co-ordination, training and representative body. They offered help with information exchanges and events to help inform self-builders, ran practical DIY seminars and information on energy saving, and offered advice on design and cost management in respect of these issues for some of the projects.

The city, for its part, recognised that by empowering this organisation with embedded local officials—dealing with planning, road and building standards as advisers—Forum Vauban could shorten the time it took to review the multiplicity of individual and group building proposals. In fact this organisation went on to drive standards for design, green space, amenity and social policy and energy efficiency, where they were particularly successful. There are over 50 passive houses and at least 100 units with Plus-Energy standards. The completed projects generally exceed the pretty strict energy criteria originally set down in the development plan organised by the City.

Vauban, housing

One of the development goals at Vauban is the creation of a variety of housing, catering for a balance of social groups. One of the drivers for this was the creation of Baugruppen: small, one-off co-operatives set up to build together. Several households get together, decide on a plot of land to purchase within the master plan, often hiring an architect and building team to assist in the design and construction process. The cost savings generated by this co-development approach—in terms of fees, economies of scale and building materials—over individual self-procurement allowed larger numbers of lower income households to participate in the scheme. Social interactions through the planning and building process help to knit community before anyone moves in. It's a sort of "bake and shake neighbourhood".

These Baugruppen in turn had the practical assistance of a Citizens' Building Stock Corporation (The Buergerbau), set-up in order to coordinate their efforts. The corporation offers a range of services throughout the project development, right up to the moment when the self-builders move into their houses. These services include guiding the building group and answering any questions during planning and contract periods, acting as centralised quantity surveyor and clerk of works, ensuring that the generally agreed standards for the scheme are met in the most efficient manner. 'Enabling' in its broadest and most constructive sense, this organisation currently manages five co-operative housing groups in the development.

What this settlement shows is a political will. Local government behaving like government: providing a lead for its citizens, enabling them, but perhaps more than these two points, trusting them to make their own decisions about what they want and need in terms of housing. Backing them and empowering them through training, helping them organise, and then letting them get on with it like a bunch of grown-ups.

Our ancestors

Local authority employees responsible for the maintenance of burial sites and representatives of the burial services industry are well aware of the situation highlighted in Ken Warpole's study "The Cemetery in the City", which indicates that British cities are running out of burial space. Articles in national newspapers by journalists such as Oliver Burkeman are beginning to bring this situation to the attention of the general public.

At the present rate, inner London cemeteries will be full within seven years. In Hackney and Tower Hamlets the crisis is worse—both boroughs have already run out of space and the London Planning Advisory Committee has reported that half of all cemeteries in London are either full or have very limited space. The problem is not confined to London. The House of Commons Environment, Transport and Regional Affairs Select Committee reports that the situation has reached crisis point in urban areas across the country.

Until primary legislation is enacted, the 1857 Burial Act will not allow for the re-use of existing graves. Cremation cannot come to our rescue: increased environmental awareness of pollution and the unsustainable nature of the process's energy requirements, plus the reluctance of some communities to employ this method of disposal on religious or cultural grounds, mean that the space put aside for burial will be at a greater premium in the foreseeable future.

The disposal, commemoration and situation of our ancestors does not seem to exercise our politicians in quite the manner many of us might wish. Promised Home Office proposals have yet to materialise. The dead do not vote and we, as a culture, are so distanced from our dead that no great public pressure has built up to combat this lack of political will. How did we get into this pickle?

The nineteenth century in Britain saw a fundamental shift in attitudes to the geographic positioning of the necropolis in relation to the rapidly expanding, densely packed metropolises of the mid-industrial revolution. Neglect, overcrowding and malpractice had rendered the local churchyard—the traditional sites of burial—both unsightly, and unsanitary.

Large suburban Victorian cemeteries, such as Brookwood London Necropolis, represent one of the better responses to this crisis of space. This example was opened some one hundred and forty years ago, set in three hundred acres of Surrey countryside and was connected to the city by means of the London South Western Railway, with a dedicated funeral station located on Westminster Bridge Road. A contemporary account in The Spectator described the Necropolis in the following terms: "The grounds of the London Necropolis are laid out with skill and taste, and present an aspect which will render it, like Père la Chaise of Paris, and some of the beautiful cemeteries in Germany, not only a sacred fane in the eyes of survivors, but an object of reverential interest to strangers and foreigners visiting the metropolis." So long as sufficient room remained to bury people, the economic structure of the joint stock ventures that developed and ran these sites of piety and genteel recreation could survive. As they became full, they were taken over by their local municipalities. Westminster Council's ill-judged sale of some of its cemeteries attests to our politicians wish to be rid of the expense of maintaining such places.

At Mæ we believe that this retreat to the suburbs is at the root of many of our culture's problems with mortality. An out-of-sight attitude has tended to keep our relationship with our ancestors out of mind. Death is not seen as a part of the cycle of creation, offering a chance to re-evaluate human and social relationships, so much as an appalling interruption and final end of an individual's life.

The vandalised state of many of our cemeteries perhaps bears witness to the distance and fear experienced by many young people when confronting death. The working out of this fear manifesting itself in destructive desecration.

If one knew people who were buried in a local cemetery, if the cemetery could help to foster local identity, how different might our attitudes towards our and others mortality be. More burial sites, more local and intimate burial sites, in many ways imitating the small churchyard pre-nineteenth century would seem to be a solution.

The American historian Lewis Mumford argued that the city of the dead actually predated the city of the living. As he wrote in The City in History: "The dead were the first to have permanent dwelling… the city of the dead is the forerunner, almost the core, of every living city." The idea "no cemetery—no city", could be expressed as "no cemetery—no civilisation".

Throughout history the manner in which people dispose of their dead represents the highest ambition of any society. Let's not race down the motorway in pursuit of the undertaker's hearse just to get to a plot of land that we and perhaps our dead friend has no connection with. Why can't we walk, or if not walk, at least have an idea were the cemetery might be located? Our involvement might then have a chance to rise from that of spectator to participant in an important social rite of passage.

Slightly shorter periods of tenure for graves will help with lack of space and ensure that a person always has access to his or her local place of internment. As Sue Gill and John Fox of The Dead Good

Funerals Guide put it: "Better a shorter period of time in a known and local setting, at the centre of the community, than an eternity on the ring road."

Our proposal for a urban cemetery takes some of its formal design cues from recent European cemetery buildings, which call upon the continent's history of the communal mausoleum—projects such as David Chipperfield Architect's work extending the burial island of San Michele in Venice and Enric Miralles's Igualada Cemetery in Barcelona.

This essentially metropolitan form is tempered in our proposal for a City Cemetery, with the inclusion of a commemorative garden, which might form the site of rites of celebration and remembrance on the roof. This landscape is joined to the surrounding landscape by a grassed ramp. By the displacement of individual internment structures, garden walkways can be produced on small city sites, or gentle curves imitating ancient burial mounds in more open landscape settings.

Using a similar typology of structures, small city sites such as railway verges or embankments, or perhaps the edges of golf courses in the suburbs, might be transformed into important contemplative and recreational places.

The paved cuts between these gardens allow space for memorial plaques and a pavement-level columbarium. These spaces are

Igualada Cemetery

City Cemetery, proposal

Our ancestors

open to the sky but protected by over-hanging planters for memorial bushes and small trees, it is envisaged that the strong grid formed by the openings of individual burial chambers will be enlivened by a great variation in individual plaques placed there. The choice of plants and freedom with the individual design of plaques and pavement memorials would, over time, start to reinforce the local character of the structure and garden complex.

The model informed the cemetery that we designed at Wilbury Hills on the edge of Letchworth Garden City. Whilst the commission was not urban, the brief showed similar social aspirations for a cemetery that would directly serve the community in which it was developed. The project included landscape burial for 9000 plus mausoleum buildings for a further 200 to address the needs of the local Italian community and to accommodate a chapel of rest.

Wilbury Hills Cemetery, mausolea

The relationship between the rural setting and the proximity of the historically important Garden City of Letchworth was the starting point for the proposed site development. The first phase of the project forms a hinge between the open field plots to the north and east and the more domestic scale of the gardens and verges of Letchworth.

It was decided early on in the design process that the remnants of traditional country forms and boundaries on site would be renovated and incorporated into the design of the project. External areas take their inspiration from the field pattern, bordered by hedges or sometimes copses of trees, of the surrounding landscape. These form a variety of spaces of differing character, some forested, some meadows, some lawns. The boundary of the site is formed by extending an existing hawthorn hedge.

Site tree planting takes three basic forms, starting with "the tree that got away" or the lone tree in a hawthorn hedge or copse. The second planting form creates screens of light trees such as birch to form some wind shelter and informal divisions of space. The third form is "trees as crop", the forest whose edges are defined by field boundaries—these formal planted blocks form a forest burial area on site.

The chapel and mausoleum block mediates between a more formal public space that faces the town and the more rural landscape beyond. Whilst an homage to Erik Gunnar Asplund's Woodland Chapel may be evident in our building, we were also interested in how seventeenth century chapels of North West Europe—as illustrated in Hendrick van Vliet's painting The New Church at Delft, from 1667—served both social and religious functions. The Church, as a social space, was visited by almost every member of the surrounding population at least once a week. It is the last period when we see a church building forming the central urban stage. Not only for religious congregation but also as a space for the display and celebration of the rich and complex interplay of nearly all of the groups and social subsets represented in the surrounding city.

The New Church at Delft, Hendrick van Vliet

The image is interesting partly because it is not painted during a religious service. We see, furthest away, some men looking at the floor of a side chapel, perhaps reading a floor marker commemorating one of the people interned below. The middle ground shows a group of gentlemen and a lady chatting and looking at the various monuments as they wander the building. They are so relaxed about their occupancy that their dog has accompanied them into the building. As far as they are concerned, this is a public square.

At Wilbury, the aspirations are more modest but the building, as a non-denominational chapel, is used as a classroom for the local school for nature studies, as well as prayer and celebration space for families. Its form takes cues from local agricultural buildings. The main hall is set at a slight angle to the volume of the administrative building; this shift in geometry references the way in which black timber barns in the region are grouped together. The highest point of the building is the roof of the entrance hall, which acts as an orientation point for the site. A large porch offers a generous space for congregations to gather on reaching the building threshold. On entering a visitor has a view across a small courtyard to the landscape beyond as well as into the chapel.

The aspiration is that the cemetery fulfils a social function with the landscape, acting as part of the town's wider green spaces strategy and operating as a local park. A loved and cared-for local cemetery might start to foster communal activities, such as the Chinese practice of gathering the family together to eat at and tend the grave site of a loved and honoured relative. Alongside the chapel, which serves as a community building, the aim is to restore the city of the dead as a place of contemplation, remembrance, recreation and even joy.

Wilbury Hills Cemetery, chapel of rest

Image credits

Habitat
(Original essay for Places for Strangers)

8   Hedrich Blessing / Chicago Historical
     Society / VIEW
9   Restored plan of the Agora at the end of
     the 5th C BC: J Travlos
9   Palazzo Chiericati Image: Domus 608,
     July/ Aug 1980, courtesy Editoriale
     Domus Spa Rozzano Milano Italy
11   Casa de la Marina plan: Matthew Farrer
12   Casa de la Marina Interior: COAC
12   Letchworth Plan: Purdom 1913,42
13   Villa Müller: Albertina, Vienna

Type
(Adapted from an article for London Festival
of Architecture, 2008, updated 2013)

17   Georgian terrace: Random House
18   Britz Metropolitan Development:
     Gareth Gardner

Place
(Adapted from lecture given at Martin Centre,
University of Cambridge)

27   City Figure Ground Plans:
     Kingston University, School of architecture
     and landscape. Postgraduate studio
     taught by Daniel Rosbottom and
     Andrew Houlton 2011/12
30   Tybalds Estate CGI: Forbes Massie
33   Agar Grove CGI: Forbes Massie

Conversation

39   Hammond Court: Tim Soar
48   Lisson Grove CGI: Forbes Massie
55   Aberdeen Park: Darbourne and Darke
61   Marquess Estate: Darbourne and Darke
62   Alexandra Road: Martin Charles,
     Architectural Press Archive/RIBA Library
     Photographs Collection.
65   Agar Grove CGI: Forbes Massie

Image section

67– David Grandorge
98

Conversation (cont.)

99– M-house: Morley von Sternberg
100
102 Lift-up House: Kilian O'Sullivan
120 Agar Grove CGI: Forbes Massie
128 Tybalds Estate CGI: Forbes Massie

Identity
(Adapted from an article for Blueprint, March
2004, updated 2014)

The State
(Adapted from articles for Architects' Journal,
July 2009 and March 2013)

140 Great Fire Etching: Museum of London
145 Jefferson Land Ordinance Grid:
     Routledge & Kegan Paul

Society
(Adapted from a lecture to the DIY Urbanism
Forum 2004)

Our Ancestors
(Adapted from Article for the Journal of
Burialand Cremation Administration, 2006
updated 2014)

159 Igualada cemetery: Sam Turner
161 The New Church at Delft,
     Hendrick Van Vliet: Lichtenstein Museum,
     Vienna
162 Wilbury Hills: David Grandorge

All other photos and drawings
by Mæ LLP

Biographies

Alex Ely is partner of Mæ. He is an Architect and Chartered Town Planner. Alex leads the award winning London based practice Mæ. The practice is involved in architecture, urban design, policy development and cultural analysis. He lectures internationally and has taught at the Sir John Cass Faculty of Art, Architecture and Design, London Metropolitan University and The University of Greenwich.

Michael Howe is an Architect and Senior Lecture at the University of Brighton and previously Co-ordinator of technology at the University of Greenwich. He was a founding member of Mæ and continues to engage with the cultural thinking of the practice.

Shumi Bose is a writer and editor and teaches History and Theory of Architecture at the Architectural Association and University of the Arts London Central St Martins. Shumi held the position of curatorial collaborator for Common Ground, the main exhibition at the Venice Biennale of Architecture in 2012 directed by Sir David Chipperfield and was co-editor of Common Ground: A Critical Reader.

David Grandorge is a photographer and academic. His work has been published and exhibited internationally, including the Prague Biennale of 2005, the Venice Architecture Biennales of 2008 and 2012, at Rake Visningrom in Trondheim, Norway and Peter von Kant gallery London. He is Senior lecturer in Structure, Construction and Materials at the Sir John Cass Faculty of Art, Architecture and Design, London Metropolitan University.

Places for strangers
by Mæ architects

Edited by
Shumi Bose

Designed by
OK-RM, London

Printed by
Push Print

Distributed by
Park Books

Park Books
Verlag Scheidegger & Spiess
Niederdorfstrasse 54
8001 Zurich, Switzerland
www.park-books.com

Available in the USA through
University of Chicago Press
press.uchicago.edu

Despite intensive research it was not possible to identify and contact copyright holders in all cases. Justifiable claims will be honoured within the parameters of customary agreements.

First edition © 2014
Mæ LLP, London
and Park Books, Zurich.

All rights reserved. No part of this publication may be reproduced in any form or by any means without the prior permission in writing from the publisher.

© of the text: Mæ LLP
© of the photographs:
   the authors
© of the images: the authors
© of the design: OK-RM

Mæ LLP
www.mae-llp.co.uk
ISBN 978-3-906027-40-1